The Signature of All Things

T0349397

Translated by Luca D'Isanto with Kevin Attell

The Signature of All Things

On Method

Giorgio Agamben

ZONE BOOKS · NEW YORK

2009

Originally published as *Signatura rerum: Sul metodo*
© 2008 Bollati Boringhieri editore.

Distributed by Princeton University Press,
Princeton, New Jersey, and Woodstock, United Kingdom

Library of Congress Cataloging-in-Publication Data

Agamben, Giorgio, 1942–
      [Signatura rerum. English]
      The signature of all things : on method / Giorgio
Agamben ; translated by Luca D'Isanto with Kevin Attell.
            p.   cm.
      Includes bibliographical references and index.
      ISBN 978-1-945861-00-0
      1. Methodology. 2. Paradigm (Theory of knowledge)
3. Foucault, Michel, 1926–1984. I. Title.
      BD241.A3513 2009
      195–dc22
                              2009001976

Contents

Preface

Anyone familiar with research in the human sciences knows that, contrary to common opinion, a reflection on method usually follows practical application, rather than preceding it. It is a matter, then, of ultimate or penultimate thoughts, to be discussed among friends and colleagues, which can legitimately be articulated only after extensive research.

The three essays published here contain my observations on three specific questions regarding method: the concept of the paradigm, the theory of signatures, and the relation between history and archaeology. If these observations appear to be investigations on the method of Michel Foucault, a scholar from whom I have learned a great deal in recent years, this is because one of the methodological principles not discussed in the book — and which I owe to Walter Benjamin — is that doctrine may legitimately be exposed only in the form of interpretation. The astute reader will be able to determine what in the three essays can be attributed to Foucault, to the author, or to both. Contrary to common opinion, method shares with logic its inability to separate itself completely from its context. There is no method that would be valid for every domain, just as there is no logic that can set aside its objects.

According to another methodological principle — also not discussed in this book — which I often make use of, the genuine philosophical element in every work, whether it be a work of art, of science, or of thought, is its capacity to be developed, which Ludwig Feuerbach defined as *Entwicklungsfähigkeit*. It is precisely when one follows such a principle that the difference between what belongs to the author of a work and what is attributable to the interpreter becomes as essential as it is difficult to grasp. I have therefore preferred to take the risk of attributing to the texts of others what began its elaboration with them, rather than run the reverse risk of appropriating thoughts or research paths that do not belong to me.

Moreover, every inquiry in the human sciences — including the present reflection on method — should entail an archaeological vigilance. In other words, it must retrace its own trajectory back to the point where something remains obscure and unthematized. Only a thought that does not conceal its own unsaid — but consantly takes it up and elaborates it — may eventually lay claim to originality.

CHAPTER ONE

What Is a Paradigm?

I

In the course of my research, I have written on certain figures such as *homo sacer*, the *Muselmann*, the state of exception, and the concentration camp. While these are all actual historical phenomena, I nonetheless treated them as paradigms whose role was to constitute and make intelligible a broader historical-problematic context. Because this approach has generated a few misunderstandings, especially for those who thought, in more or less good faith, that my intention was to offer merely historiographical theses or reconstructions, I must pause here and reflect on the meaning and function of the use of paradigms in philosophy and the human sciences.

Foucault frequently used the term "paradigm" in his writings, even though he never defined it precisely. Nonetheless, in *The Archaeology of Knowledge* and subsequent works, in order to distinguish the objects of his investigations from those of the historical disciplines, he designated them with terms like "positivity," "problematization," "discursive formation," "apparatus," and, more generally, "knowledge." In a May 1978 lecture at the Société Française de Philosophie, he defines "knowledge" thus: "The use of the word knowledge (*savoir*) . . . refers to all procedures and all effects of knowledge (*connaissance*) which are acceptable at a given point in time and in a specific domain." In order to clarify the necessary relation of the concept of knowledge to that of power,

Foucault added these comments: "For nothing can exist as an element of knowledge if, on one hand, it does not conform to a set of rules and constraints characteristic, for example, of a given type of scientific discourse in a given period, and if, on the other hand, it does not possess the effects of coercion or simply the incentives peculiar to what is scientifically validated or simply rational or simply generally accepted."[1]

As others have noted, these concepts are analogous to Thomas S. Kuhn's notion of "scientific paradigms," introduced in his book, *The Structure of Scientific Revolutions*. Hubert Dreyfus and Paul Rabinow, for example, argue that although Foucault never thematized the function of paradigms, "his current work clearly follows a course that uses these insights, if not the words themselves. He is now proceeding through a description of discourse as the historical articulation of a paradigm, and approaching analytics in a manner that is heavily dependent on the isolation and description of social paradigms and their practical applications."[2]

Yet Foucault, who declared that he had read Kuhn's "admirable and definitive" book only after he had completed *The Order of Things*, almost never refers to it, and even seems to distance himself from Kuhn.[3] In his 1978 introduction to the American edition of Georges Canguilhem's *The Normal and the Pathological*, Foucault writes: "This norm cannot be identified with a theoretical structure or an actual paradigm because today's scientific truth is itself only an episode of it—let us say provisional at most. It is not by depending on a 'normal science' in T. S. Kuhn's sense that one can return to the past and validly trace its history: it is rediscovering the 'norm' process, the actual knowledge of which is only one moment of it."[4]

It is therefore necessary first of all to reflect on whether the analogy between these two different methods does not correspond to different problems, strategies, and inquiries and whether the "paradigm" of Foucault's archaeology is not merely a homonym for that which, according to Kuhn, marks the emergence of scientific revolutions.

2

Kuhn recognized that he had used the concept of "paradigm" in two different senses.[5] The first meaning of "paradigm," which he proposes to replace with the term "disciplinary matrix," designates the common possessions of the members of a certain scientific community, namely, the set of techniques, models, and values to which the group members more or less consciously adhere. The second meaning refers to a single element within the set, such as Isaac Newton's *Principia* or Ptolemy's *Almagest*, that serves as a common example and thus replaces explicit rules and permits the formulation of a specific and coherent tradition of inquiry.

When Kuhn elaborated on Ludwik Fleck's concept of "thought style" (*Denkstil*) and the distinction between what is and what is not pertinent within a "thought collective" (*Denkkollektiv*), he sought, through the concept of the paradigm, to examine what makes possible the constitution of a normal science, that is, a science capable of determining which problems within a specific community are scientific or not. Normal science does not then mean one governed by a precise and coherent system of rules. On the contrary, if the rules are derived from paradigms, then paradigms can "determine normal science" even in the absence of rules.[6] This is the second meaning of the concept of paradigm, which Kuhn considers "most novel:"[7] a paradigm is simply an example, a single case that by its repeatability acquires the capacity to model tacitly the behavior and research practices of scientists. The empire of the rule, understood as the canon of scientificity, is thus replaced by that of the paradigm; the universal logic of the law is replaced by the specific and singular logic of the example. And when an old paradigm is replaced by a new paradigm that is no longer compatible with the previous one, what Kuhn calls a scientific revolution occurs.

3

Foucault constantly sought to abandon traditional analyses of power that were grounded on juridical and institutional models as well as on universal categories (of law, the state, the theory of sovereignty). He focused instead on the concrete mechanisms through which power penetrates the very bodies of subjects and thereby governs their forms of life. Here the analogy with Kuhn's paradigms seems to find an important corroboration. Just as Kuhn set aside the identification and examination of the rules constituting a normal science in order to focus on the paradigms that determine scientists' behavior, Foucault questioned the traditional primacy of the juridical models of the theory of power in order to bring to the fore multiple disciplines and political techniques through which the state integrates the care of the life of individuals within its confines. And just as Kuhn separated normal science from the system of rules that define it, Foucault frequently distinguished "normalization," which characterizes disciplinary power, from the juridical system of legal procedures.

If the proximity of these two methods seems clear, then it is all the more enigmatic why Foucault remained silent when it came to Kuhn's work and seems to have carefully avoided using the very term "paradigm" in the The Archaeology of Knowledge. To be sure, the reasons for Foucault's silence may have been personal. In his reply to George Steiner, who had reproached him for not mentioning Kuhn by name, Foucault explains that he had read Kuhn's book only after he had completed The Order of Things and adds: "I therefore did not cite Kuhn, but the historian of science who molded and inspired his thought: Georges Canguilhem."[8]

This statement is surprising, to say the least, since Kuhn, who did acknowledge in the preface to *The Structure of Scientific Revolutions* his debt to two French epistemologists, Alexandre Koyré and Émile Meyerson, does not once mention Canguilhem in the book. Since Foucault must have meant what he said, perhaps his close relationship to Canguilhem prompted him to repay Kuhn for this discourtesy. However, even if Foucault was not above holding personal grudges, this alone cannot explain his silence concerning Kuhn.

4

A closer reading of Foucault's writings shows that even without naming the American epistemologist, he did on more than one occasion grapple with Kuhn's notion of paradigm. In "Truth and Power," Foucault's 1976 interview with Alessandro Fontana and Pasquale Pasquino, when answering a question concerning the notion of discontinuity, he explicitly opposed his notion of the "discursive regime" to that of the paradigm:

> Thus, it is not a change of content (refutation of old errors, recovery of old truths), nor is it a change of theoretical form (renewal of a paradigm, modification of systematic ensembles). It is a question of what *governs* statements, and the way in which they *govern* each other so as to constitute a set of propositions that are scientifically acceptable and, hence, capable of being verified or falsified by scientific procedures. In short, there is a problem of the regime, the politics of the scientific statement. At this level, it's not so much a matter of knowing what external power imposes itself on science as of what effects of power circulate among scientific statements, what constitutes, as it were, their internal regime of power, and how and why at certain moments that regime undergoes a global modification.[9]

A few lines later, when referring to *The Order of Things*, he insists on the distance between a discursive regime (a genuine political phenomenon) and a paradigm (a criterion of scientific truth): "What was lacking here was this problem of the 'discursive regime,' of the effects of power peculiar to the play of statements. I confused this too much with systematicity, theoretical form, or something like a paradigm."[10] At some point, then, Foucault did indeed recognize the proximity to Kuhn's paradigm; but this proximity was not the effect of an actual affinity but the result of a certain confusion. What was decisive for Foucault was the movement of the paradigm from epistemology to politics, its shift onto the plane of a politics of statements and discursive regimes, where it was not so much the "change of theoretical form" that was in question as the "internal regime of power," which determines the way in which the statements govern one another to constitute an ensemble.

From this perspective, it is clear that even though he does not explicitly name them in *The Archaeology of Knowledge*, Foucault already wished to distinguish the theme of his own research from Kuhn's paradigms. For Foucault, discursive formations do not define

> the state of knowledge at a given moment in time: they do not draw up a list of what, from that moment, had been demonstrated to be true and had assumed the status of definitively acquired knowledge, and a list of what, on the other hand, had been accepted without either proof or adequate demonstration, or of what had been accepted as a common belief or a belief demanded by the power of the imagination. To analyze positivities is to show in accordance with which rules a discursive practice may form groups of objects, enunciations, concepts, or theoretical choices."[11]

A little further down, Foucault describes something that seems to correspond to Kuhn's paradigm but that he prefers to

call "epistemological figures" or "thresholds of epistemologization." Thus he writes: "When in the operation of a discursive formation, a group of statements is articulated, claims to validate
(even unsuccessfully) norms of verification and coherence, and
when it exercises a dominant function (as a model, a critique,
or a verification) over knowledge, we will say that the discursive formation crosses a *threshold of epistemologization*. When the
epistemological figure thus outlined obeys a number of formal
criteria. . . ."[12]

The change in terminology is not merely formal: in a manner
wholly consistent with the premises of *The Archaeology of Knowledge*, Foucault diverts attention from the criteria that permit the
constitution of a normal science with respect to subjects (the
members of a scientific community) to the pure occurrence of
"groups of statements" and "figures," independently of any reference to subjects ("a group of statements is articulated," "the
epistemological figure thus outlined"). And when, a propos of
the different types of history of science, Foucault defines his own
concept of the episteme, it is once again not a matter of identifying something like a worldview or a structure of thought that
imposes common postulates and norms on the subject. Rather,
the episteme is the "total set of relations that unite, at a given
period, the discursive practices that give rise to epistemological figures, sciences, and possibly formalized systems."[13] Unlike
Kuhn's paradigm, the episteme does not define what is knowable
in a given period, but what is implicit in the fact that a given discourse or epistemological figure exists at all: "In the enigma of
scientific discourse, what the analysis of the episteme questions is
not its right to be a science, but the fact that it exists."[14]

The Archaeology of Knowledge has been read as a manifesto of
historiographical discontinuity. Whether this characterization
is correct or not (Foucault contested it a number of times), it
is certain that in this book Foucault appears most interested in

that which permits the constitution of contexts and groups, in the positive existence of "figures" and series. Only that these contexts emerge in accordance with an entirely peculiar epistemological model which coincides neither with those commonly accepted in historical research nor with Kuhnian paradigms, and which we must therefore undertake to identify.

5

Consider the notion of panopticism, which Foucault presents in the third part of *Discipline and Punish*. The panopticon is a particular historical phenomenon, an architectural model published by Jeremy Bentham in Dublin in 1791 under the title *Panopticon; or, The Inspection-House: Containing the Idea of a New Principle of Construction, Applicable to Any Sort of Establishment, in Which Persons of Any Description Are to Be Kept Under Inspection.* Foucault recalls its basic features:

> We know the principle on which it was based: at the periphery, an annular building; at the centre, a tower; this tower is pierced with wide windows that open onto the inner side of the ring; the peripheric building is divided into cells, each of which extends the whole width of the building; they have two windows, one on the inside, corresponding to the windows of the tower; the other, on the outside, allows the light to cross the cell from one end to the other. All that is needed, then, is to place a supervisor in a central tower and to shut up in each cell a madman, a patient, a condemned man, a worker or a schoolboy. By the effect of backlighting, one can observe from the tower, standing out precisely against the light, the small captive shadows in the cells of the periphery. They are like so many cages, so many small theatres.[5]

Yet for Foucault, the panopticon is both a "generalizable model of functioning," namely "panopticism," that is to say, the principle of an "ensemble," and the "panoptic modality of power." As such, it is a "figure of political technology that may and must be detached from any specific use"; it is not merely a "dream building," but "the diagram of a mechanism of power reduced to its ideal form."[16] In short, the panopticon functions as a paradigm in the strict sense: it is a singular object that, standing equally for all others of the same class, defines the intelligibility of the group of which it is a part and which, at the same time, it constitutes. Anyone who has read *Discipline and Punish* knows not only how the panopticon, situated as it is at the end of the section on discipline, performs a decisive strategic function for the understanding of the disciplinary modality of power, but also how it becomes something like the epistemological figure that, in defining the disciplinary universe of modernity, also marks the threshold over which it passes into the societies of control.

This is not an isolated case in Foucault's work. On the contrary, one could say that in this sense paradigms define the most characteristic gesture of Foucault's method. The great confinement, the confession, the investigation, the examination, the care of the self: these are all singular historical phenomena that Foucault treats as paradigms, and this is what constitutes his specific intervention into the field of historiography. Paradigms establish a broader problematic context that they both constitute and make intelligible.

Daniel S. Milo has remarked that Foucault demonstrates the relevance of contexts produced by metaphorical fields in contrast to those created only through chronological caesurae.[17] Following the orientations of such works as Marc Bloch's *Royal Touch*, Ernst Kantorowicz's *King's Two Bodies*, and Lucien Febvre's *Problem of Unbelief in the Sixteenth Century*, Foucault is said to have freed historiography from the exclusive domain of metonymic contexts—for example, the eighteenth-century or southern France—in order to return metaphorical contexts to primacy.

This observation is correct only if one keeps in mind that for Foucault, it is a question not of metaphors but of paradigms in the sense noted above. Paradigms obey not the logic of the metaphorical transfer of meaning but the analogical logic of the example. Here we are not dealing with a signifier that is extended to designate heterogeneous phenomena by virtue of the same semantic structure; more akin to allegory than to metaphor, the paradigm is a singular case that is isolated from its context only insofar as, by exhibiting its own singularity, it makes intelligible a new ensemble, whose homogeneity it itself constitutes. That is to say, to give an example is a complex act which supposes that the term functioning as a paradigm is deactivated from its normal use, not in order to be moved into another context but, on the contrary, to present the canon—the rule—of that use, which can not be shown in any other way.

Sextus Pompeius Festus informs us that the Romans distinguished *exemplar* from *exemplum*. The exemplar can be observed by the senses *(oculis conspicitur)* and refers to that which one must imitate *(exemplar est quod simile faciamus)*. The *exemplum*, on the other hand, demands a more complex evaluation (which is not merely sensible: *animo aestimatur)*; its meaning is above all moral and intellectual. The Foucauldian paradigm is both of these things: not only an exemplar and model, which imposes the constitution of a normal science, but also and above all an *exemplum*, which allows statements and discursive practices to be gathered into a new intelligible ensemble and in a new problematic context.

6

The *locus classicus* of the epistemology of the example is in Aristotle's *Prior Analytics*. There, Aristotle distinguishes the procedure by way of paradigms from induction and deduction. "It is clear," he writes, "that the paradigm does not function as a part with respect to the whole [*hôs meros pros holon*], nor as a whole with respect to the part [*hôs holon pros meros*], but as a part with respect to the part [*hôs meros pros meros*], if both are under the same but one is better known than the other."[18] That is to say, while induction proceeds from the particular to the universal and deduction from the universal to the particular, the paradigm is defined by a third and paradoxical type of movement, which goes from the particular to the particular. The example constitutes a peculiar form of knowledge that does not proceed by articulating together the universal and the particular, but seems to dwell on the plane of the latter. Aristotle's treatment of the paradigm does not move beyond these brief observations, and the status of knowledge resting within the particular is not examined any further. Not only does Aristotle seem to hold that the common type exists before particulars, but he leaves undefined the status of "greater knowability" (*gnôrimôteron*) that belongs to the example.

The epistemological status of the paradigm becomes clear only if we understand — making Aristotle's thesis more radical — that it calls into question the dichotomous opposition between the particular and the universal which we are used to seeing as inseparable from procedures of knowing, and presents instead a singularity irreducible to any of the dichotomy's two terms. The domain of his discourse is not logic but analogy, the theory of which was reconstructed by Enzo Melandri in a book that has by now become a classic. And the *analogon* it produces is neither particular nor general. Hence its special value, and our task of understanding it.

7

In *La linea e il circolo*, Melandri shows that analogy is opposed to the dichotomous principle dominating Western logic. Against the drastic alternative "A or B," which excludes the third, analogy imposes its *tertium datur*, its stubborn "neither A nor B." In other words, analogy intervenes in the dichotomies of logic (particular/ universal; form/content; lawfulness/exemplarity; and so on) not to take them up into a higher synthesis but to transform them into a force field traversed by polar tensions, where (as in an electromagnetic field) their substantial identities evaporate. But in what sense and in what way is the third given here? Certainly not as a term homogeneous with the first two, the identity of which could in turn be defined by a binary logic. Only from the point of view of dichotomy can analogy (or paradigm) appear as *tertium comparationis*. The analogical third is attested here above all through the disidentification and neutralization of the first two, which now become indiscernible. The third is this indiscernibility, and if one tries to grasp it by means of bivalent caesurae, one necessarily runs up against an undecidable. It is thus impossible to clearly separate an example's paradigmatic character—its standing for all cases—from the fact that it is one case among others. As in a magnetic field, we are dealing not with extensive and scalable magnitudes but with vectorial intensities.

8

Nowhere, perhaps, is the paradoxical relation between paradigms and generality as forcefully formulated as in *The Critique of Judgment*, where Kant conceives of the necessity of the aesthetic judgment in the form of an example for which it is impossible to state the rule:

> Now this necessity is of a special kind: not a theoretical objective necessity, where it can be cognized a priori that everyone will feel this satisfaction in the object called beautiful by me, nor a practical necessity, where by means of concepts of a pure will, serving as rules for freely acting beings, this satisfaction is a necessary

consequence of an objective law and signifies nothing other than that one absolutely (without a further aim) ought to act in a certain way. Rather, as a necessity that is thought in an aesthetic judgment, it can only be called exemplary [*exemplarisch*], i.e., a necessity of the assent of all to a judgment that is regarded as an example [*Beispiel*] of a universal rule that one cannot produce [*angeben*].[19]

As with the aesthetic judgment for Kant, a paradigm actually presupposes the impossibility of the rule; but if the rule is missing or cannot be formulated, from where will the example draw its probative value? And how is it possible to supply the examples of an unassignable rule?

The aporia may be resolved only if we understand that a paradigm implies the total abandonment of the particular-general couple as the model of logical inference. The rule (if it is still possible to speak of rules here) is not a generality preexisting the singular cases and applicable to them, nor is it something resulting from the exhaustive enumeration of specific cases. Instead, it is the exhibition alone of the paradigmatic case that constitutes a rule, which as such cannot be applied or stated.

9

Anyone familiar with the history of the monastic orders knows that, at least in regard to the first centuries, it is difficult to understand the status of what the documents call *regula*. In the most ancient testimonies, *regula* simply means *conversatio fratrum*, the monks' way of life in a given monastery. It is often identified with the founder's way of living envisaged as *forma vitae* — that is, as an example to be followed. And the founder's life is in turn the sequel to the life of Jesus as narrated in the Gospels. With the gradual development of the monastic orders, and the Roman Curia's growing need to exercise control over them, the term *regula* increasingly assumed the meaning of a written text, preserved in the monastery, which had to be read by the person who, having embraced the monastic life, consented to subject himself to the prescriptions and prohibitions contained therein. However, at least until Saint Benedict, the rule does not indicate a general norm but the living community (*koinos bios, cenobio*) that results from an example and in which the life of each monk tends at the limit to become paradigmatic—that is, to constitute itself as *forma vitae*.

We can therefore say, joining Aristotle's observations with those of Kant, that a paradigm entails a movement that goes from singularity to singularity and, without ever leaving singularity, transforms every singular case into an *exemplar* of a general rule that can never be stated a priori.

10

In 1947, Victor Goldschmidt, an author whom Foucault appears to have known and admired, published *Le paradigme dans la dialectique platonicienne*. As is often the case with the writings of this brilliant historian of philosophy, the examination of an apparently marginal problem—the use of examples in Plato's dialogues—throws new light on the entirety of Plato's thought, especially the relation between ideas and the sensible, of which the paradigm is revealed to be the technical expression. Georges Rodier had already observed that sometimes ideas function in the dialogues as paradigms for sensible objects, whereas at other times sensible objects are presented as the paradigms of ideas. If in the *Euthyphro* the idea of piety is that which is used as a paradigm in order to understand corresponding sensible objects, in the *Statesman* a sensible paradigm—weaving—instead leads to the understanding of ideas. To explain how an example may produce knowledge, Plato introduces here the example of the syllables children are able to recognize in different words as a "paradigm for the paradigm": "A paradigm is generated when an entity, which is found in something other and separated [*diespasmenôi*; the Greek term means "torn," "lacerated"] in another entity, is judged correctly and recognized as the same, and having been reconnected together generates a true and unique opinion concerning each and both."[20]

Commenting on this definition, Goldschmidt shows that here there seems to be a paradoxical structure, at once sensible and mental, which he calls the "element-form."[21] In other words, even though it is a singular sensible phenomenon, the paradigm somehow contains the *eidos*, the very form that is to be defined. It is not a simple sensible element that is present in two different places, but something like a relation between the sensible and the mental, the element and the form ("the paradigmatic element is itself a relationship").[22] Just as in the case of recollection—which Plato often uses as a paradigm for knowledge—where a sensible phenomenon is placed into a nonsensible relation with itself, and thus re-cognized in the other, so in the paradigm it is a matter not of corroborating a certain sensible likeness but of producing it by means of an operation. For this reason, the paradigm is never already given, but is generated and produced (*paradeigmatos . . . genesis; paradeigmata . . . gignomena*) by "placing alongside," "conjoining together," and above all by "showing" and "exposing" (*paraballontas . . . paratithemena . . . endeiknynai . . . deichthêi . . . deichthenta*).[23] The paradigmatic relation does not merely occur between sensible objects or between these objects and a general rule; it occurs instead between a singularity (which thus becomes a paradigm) and its exposition (its intelligibility).

II

Consider the relatively simple case of a grammatical example. Grammar is constituted and may state its rules only through the practice of paradigmatics, by exhibiting linguistic examples. But what is the use of language that defines grammatical practice? How is a grammatical example produced? Take the case of the paradigms that in Latin grammars account for the declensions of nouns. Through its paradigmatic exhibition (*rosa*, *ros-ae*, *ros-ae*, *ros-am* . . .), the normal use as well as the denotative character of the term "rose" is suspended. The term thus makes possible the constitution and intelligibility of the group "feminine noun of the first declension," of which it is both a member and a paradigm. What is essential here is the suspension of reference and normal use. If, in order to explain the rule that defines the class of performatives, the linguist utters the example "I swear," it is clear that this syntagma is not to be understood as the uttering of a real oath. To be capable of acting as an example, the syntagma must be suspended from its normal function, and nevertheless it is precisely by virtue of this nonfunctioning and suspension that it can show how the syntagma works and can allow the rule to be stated. If we now ask ourselves whether the rule can be applied to the example, the answer is not easy. In fact, the example is excluded from the rule not because it does not belong to the normal case but, on the contrary, because it exhibits its belonging to it. The example, then, is the symmetrical opposite of the exception: whereas the exception is included through its exclusion, the example is excluded through the exhibition of its inclusion. However, in this way, according to the etymological meaning of the Greek term, it shows "beside itself" (*paradeiknymi*) both its own intelligibility and that of the class it constitutes.

12

In Plato, the paradigm has its place in dialectics, which, by articulating the relation between the intelligible and the sensible order, makes knowledge possible. "The relation between these two orders may be conceived in two ways: as a relation of like-ness (between copy and model) or as a relation of proportion."[24] To each of these conceptions there corresponds, according to Goldschmidt, a specific dialectical procedure: to the first, recol-lection (defined by Plato in the *Meno* and in the *Theatetus*); to the second, the paradigm, which is discussed above all in the *Sophist* and in the *Statesman*. Continuing Goldschmidt's analyses we must now attempt to understand the specific meaning and function of the paradigm in dialectics. The whole thorny discussion of the dialectical method in book 6 of the *Republic* becomes clear when it is understood as an exposition of the paradigmatic method.[25] Plato distinguishes two stages or moments within the emergence of science, which are represented as two continuous segments on a straight line. The first, which defines the procedures of "geom-etry and calculus and those who practice these kinds of sciences," grounds its investigations on hypotheses. It presupposes (this is the meaning of the Greek term *hypothesis*, from *hypotithêmi*, "I lay it below as a base") givens that are treated as known prin-ciples, the evidence of which does not need to be accounted for. The second belongs to dialectics: "it does not consider hypoth-eses as first principles [*archai*] but truly as hypotheses—that is, as stepping stones to take off from, enabling it to reach the unhypo-thetical [*anypotheton*] first principle of everything. Having touched this principle, and keeping hold of what follows from it, it comes down to a conclusion without making use of anything sensible at all, but only of ideas themselves, moving on from ideas to ideas, and ending with ideas."[26]

What does it mean to treat hypotheses (presuppositions) as hypotheses rather than as principles? What is a hypothesis that is not presupposed but exposed as such? If we recall that the knowability of the paradigm is never presupposed, and that on the contrary its specific operation consists in suspending and deactivating its empirical givenness in order to exhibit only an intelligibility, then treating hypotheses as hypotheses means treating them as paradigms.

Here the aporia that both Aristotle and modern commentators have observed—that in Plato the idea is the paradigm of the sensible and the sensible the paradigm of ideas—is resolved. The idea is not another being that is presupposed by the sensible or coincides with it: it is the sensible considered as a paradigm—that is, in the medium of its intelligibility. This is why Plato is able to state that even dialectics, like the arts, starts from hypotheses (*ex hypotheseôs iousa*),[27] but unlike them it takes hypotheses as hypotheses rather than principles. To put it differently, dialectics uses hypotheses as paradigms. The non-hypothetical, to which dialectics has access, is above all opened by the paradigmatic use of the sensible. It is in this sense that we should understand the following passage, where the dialectical method is defined as "doing away with hypothesis": "Dialectic is the only method that proceeds in this manner, doing away with hypotheses [*tas hypotheseis anairousa*] and reaching to the first principle itself."[28] *Anaireô*, like its corresponding Latin term *tollere* (and the German *aufheben*, which Hegel placed at the heart of his dialectic), signifies both "to take," "to raise," and "to take away," "to eliminate." As previously noted, what operates as a paradigm is withdrawn from its normal use and, at the same time, exposed as such. The non-hypothetical is what discloses itself at the point where hypotheses are "taken away," that is, raised and eliminated at the same time. The intelligibility in which dialectics moves in its "descent toward the end" is the paradigmatic intelligibility of the sensible.

13

The hermeneutic circle, which defines the procedures of knowledge in the human sciences, acquires its true meaning only from the perspective of the paradigmatic method. Before Friedrich Daniel Ernst Schleiermacher, Georg Anton Friedrich Ast had already observed that in the philological sciences, knowledge of a single phenomenon presupposes knowledge of the whole and, vice versa, knowledge of the whole presupposes that of single phenomena. Grounding this hermeneutic circle in *Being and Time* on pre-understanding as *Dasein*'s anticipatory existential structure, Martin Heidegger helped the human sciences out of this difficulty and indeed guaranteed the "more original" character of their knowledge. Since then, the motto "What is decisive is not to get out of the circle but to come into it in the right way" has become a magic formula that allows the inquirer to transform the vicious circle into a virtuous one.[29]

However, such a guarantee was less reassuring than it at first appeared. If the activity of the interpreter is always already anticipated by a pre-understanding that is elusive, what does it mean "to come into [the circle] in the right way?" Heidegger suggested that it was a matter of never allowing the pre-understanding to be presented (*vorgeben*) by "fancies" or "popular conceptions," but instead "working [it] out in terms of the things themselves."[30] This can only mean—and the circle then seems to become even more "vicious"—that the inquirer must be able to recognize in phenomena the signature of a pre-understanding that depends on their own existential structure.

The aporia is resolved if we understand that the hermeneutic circle is in actuality a paradigmatic circle. There is no duality here between "single phenomenon" and "the whole" as there was in Ast and Schleiermacher: the whole only results from the paradigmatic exposition of individual cases. And there is no circularity, as in Heidegger, between a "before" and an "after," between pre-understanding and interpretation. In the paradigm, intelligibility does not precede the phenomenon; it stands, so to speak, "beside" it (*para*). According to Aristotle's definition, the paradigmatic gesture moves not from the particular to the whole and from the whole to the particular but from the singular to the singular. The phenomenon, exposed in the medium of its knowability, shows the whole of which it is the paradigm. With regard to phenomena, this is not a presupposition (a "hypothesis"): as a "non-presupposed principle," it stands neither in the past nor in the present but in their exemplary constellation.

14

Between 1924 and 1929, Aby Warburg was working on his "atlas of images," which was to be called *Mnemosyne.* As is well-known, it is a collection of plates or boards to which are attached a heterogeneous series of images (reproductions of works of art or manuscripts, photographs cut out of newspapers or taken by Warburg himself, and so on) often referring to a single theme that Warburg defined as *Pathosformel.* Consider plate 46, in which we find the *Pathosformel* "Nymph," the figure of a woman in movement (when she appears in Ghirlandaio's fresco in the Tornabuoni Chapel, Warburg gives her the familiar nickname Fraulein Schnellbring, "Miss Quick-Bring"). The plate is made up of twenty-seven images, each of which is somehow related to the theme that gives its name to the whole. In addition to Ghirlandaio's fresco, one can identify a Roman ivory relief, a sibyl from the cathedral of Sessa Aurunca, a few miniatures from a sixteenth-century Florentine manuscript, a detail from one of Botticelli's frescos, Fra Filippo Lippi's tondo of the Madonna and the birth of John the Baptist, a photo of a peasant woman from Settignano taken by Warburg himself, and so on. How should we read this plate? What is the relation that holds together the individual images? In other words, where is the nymph?

A mistaken way of reading the plate would be to see in it something like an iconographic repertory, where what is in question is the origin and history of the iconographic theme "figure of a woman in movement." This would be a matter of arranging, as far as possible, the individual images in chronological order by following the probable genetic relation that, binding one to the other, would eventually allow us to go back to the archetype, to the "formula of *pathos*" from which they all originate. A slightly more careful reading of the plate shows that none of the images is the original, just as none of the images is simply a copy or repetition. Just as it is impossible to distinguish between creation and performance, original and execution, in the "formulaic" composition that Milman Parry had recognized at the basis of the Homeric poems and more generally of any oral compositions, so are Warburg's *Pathosformeln* hybrids of archetype and phenomenon, first-timeness (*primavoltità*) and repetition. Every photograph is the original; every image constitutes the *archê* and is, in this sense, "archaic." But the nymph herself is neither archaic nor contemporary; she is undecidable in regards to diachrony and synchrony, unicity and multiplicity. This means that the nymph is the paradigm of which individual nymphs are the exemplars. Or to be more precise, in accordance with the constitutive ambiguity of Plato's dialectic, the nymph is the paradigm of the single images, and the single images are the paradigms of the nymph.

In other words, the nymph is an *Urphänomen*, an "originary phenomenon" in Goethe's sense of the term. This technical term, which is essential to Goethe's investigations on nature from the *Theory of Colors* to *The Metamorphosis of Plants*, even though it is never clearly defined by the author, becomes intelligible only when understood in a decidedly paradigmatic sense, thereby following a suggestion by Elizabeth Rotten, who traced its origin back to Plato. Goethe often juxtaposes his method to that which proceeds by "single cases and general rubrics, opinions and hypotheses."[31] In the essay "The Experiment as Mediator

Between Object and Subject," he proposes a model of "experience of a higher type," where the unification of individual phenomena does not occur "in hypothetical and systematic manner," but where instead each phenomenon "stands in relation with countless others, in the way we say of a freely floating luminous point, that it emits its rays in every direction."[32] How such a singular relation among phenomena ought to be understood is discussed a few lines below in a passage where the paradigmatic nature of the procedure is stated beyond any doubt: "Such an experience, which consists of many others, is clearly of a higher type. It represents the formula in which countless single examples find their expression."[33] "Every existent," he reiterates in another fragment, "is the *analogon* of every existent; for this reason, existence always appears to us as separated and connected at the same time. If one follows the analogy too closely, everything becomes identical; if we avoid it, everything scatters to infinity."[34] As a paradigm, the *Urphänomen* is thus the place where analogy lives in perfect equilibrium beyond the opposition between generality and particularity. Hence, Goethe writes of the "pure phenomenon" that it can "never be isolated, since it shows itself in a continuous series of appearances."[35] And in the *Maximen und Reflexionen*, he sums up its nature with a definition that could be equally valid for the paradigm: "the originary phenomenon: ideal insofar as it is the last knowable/real, insofar as it is known/symbolic because it embraces all cases:/identical with all cases."[36] Even though it never crosses into the generality of a hypothesis or law, the *Urphänomen* is nevertheless knowable; it is indeed in the single phenomenon the last knowable element, its capacity to constitute itself as a paradigm. For this reason, a famous Goethean dictum states that one should never look beyond the phenomena: insofar as they are paradigms, "they are theory."

15

At this point, let us try to put in the form of theses some of the features that, according to our analysis, define a paradigm:

1. A paradigm is a form of knowledge that is neither inductive nor deductive but analogical. It moves from singularity to singularity.
2. By neutralizing the dichotomy between the general and the particular, it replaces a dichotomous logic with a bipolar analogical model.
3. The paradigmatic case becomes such by suspending and, at the same time, exposing its belonging to the group, so that it is never possible to separate its exemplarity from its singularity.
4. The paradigmatic group is never presupposed by the paradigms; rather, it is immanent in them.
5. In the paradigm, there is no origin or *archê*; every phenomenon is the origin, every image archaic.
6. The historicity of the paradigm lies neither in diachrony nor in synchrony but in a crossing of the two.

At this point, I think it is clear what it means to work by way of paradigms for both me and Foucault. *Homo sacer* and the concentration camp, the *Muselmann* and the state of exception, and, more recently, the Trinitarian *oikonomia* and acclamations are not hypotheses through which I intended to explain modernity by tracing it back to something like a cause or historical origin. On the contrary, as their very multiplicity might have signaled, each time it was a matter of paradigms whose aim was to make intelligible series of phenomena whose kinship had eluded or could elude the historian's gaze. To be sure, my investigations, like those of Foucault, have an archaeological character, and the phenomena with which they deal unfold across time and therefore require an attention to documents and diachrony that cannot but follow the laws of historical philology. Nevertheless, the *archê* they reach—and this perhaps holds for all historical inquiry—is not an origin presupposed in time. Rather, locating itself at the crossing of diachrony and synchrony, it makes the inquirer's present intelligible as much as the past of his or her object. Archaeology, then, is always a paradigmatology, and the capacity to recognize and articulate paradigms defines the rank of the inquirer no less than does his or her ability to examine the documents of an archive. In the final analysis, the paradigm determines the very possibility of producing in the midst of the chronological archive—which in itself is inert—the *plans de clivage* (as French epistemologists call them) that alone make it legible.

If one asks whether the paradigmatic character lies in things themselves or in the mind of the inquirer, my response must be that the question itself makes no sense. The intelligibility in question in the paradigm has an ontological character. It refers not to the cognitive relation between subject and object but to being. There is, then, a paradigmatic ontology. And I know of no better definition of it than the one contained in a poem by Wallace Stevens titled "Description Without Place":

> It is possible that to seem—it is to be,
> As the sun is something seeming and it is.
>
> The sun is an example. What it seems
> It is and in such seeming all things are.

CHAPTER TWO

Theory of Signatures

I

Book 9 of Paracelsus's treatise *De natura rerum* (On the Nature of Things) is titled "De signatura rerum naturalium" (Concerning the Signature of Natural Things).[1] The original core of the Paracelsian episteme is the idea that all things bear a sign that manifests and reveals their invisible qualities. "Nothing is without a sign" (*Nichts ist ohn ein Zeichen*), he writes in *Von den naturlichen Dingen*, "since nature does not release anything in which it has not marked what is to be found within that thing."[2] "There is nothing exterior that is not an announcement of the interior," reads the *Liber de podagricis*, and by means of signs man can know what has been marked in each thing.[3] And if, in this sense, "all things, herbs, seeds, stones, and roots reveal in their qualities, forms, and figures [*Gestalt*] that which is in them," if "they all become known through their *signatum*," then "*signatura* is the science by which everything that is hidden is found, and without this art nothing of any profundity can be done."[4] This science, however, like all knowledge, is a consequence of sin, insofar as Adam, in Eden, was absolutely unmarked (*unbezeichnet*), and would have remained so had he not "fallen into nature," which leaves nothing unmarked.

Based on these presuppositions, "De signatura rerum naturalium" is able to go right to the heart of the matter and inquire into the nature and the number of "signers." Here *signatura* is no longer the name of a science but the very act and effect of marking: "In this book, our first business, as being about to philosophise, is with the signature of things, as, for instance, to set forth how they are signed, what signator exists, and how many signs are reckoned."[5] According to Paracelsus, there are three *signators*: man, the Archeus, and the stars (*Astra*). The signs of the stars, which make prophecies and presages possible, manifest "the supernatural force and virtue" (*übernatürliche Kraft und Tugend*) of things. The divinatory sciences — for example, geomancy, chiromancy, physiognomy, hydromancy, pyromancy, necromancy, and astronomy — examine these signs. The monsters treated by divination, such as hermaphrodites and androgynous beings, are nothing but a sign imprinted by the ascendant celestial bodies. And Paracelsus argues that not only the stars in the sky but also the "stars of the human mind" — which "perpetually at all moments, with the Phantasy, Estimations, or Imagination, rise and set just as in the firmament above"[6] — can leave their mark on the body, as happens with pregnant women whose *Fantasey* draws on the flesh of the fetus its "monstrous signs" (*Monstrosische Zeichen*).[7]

Similarly, physiognomy and chiromancy teach one how to decipher the secret of the "inner man" in the signs that the stars have imprinted on men's faces and limbs or on the lines of their hands. However, the relation between the stars and men is not merely one of unilateral subjection. Paracelsus writes:

> The wise man can dominate the stars, and is not subject to them. Nay, the stars are subject to the wise man, and are forced to obey him, not he the stars. The stars compel and coerce the animal man, so that where they lead he must follow, just as a thief does the gallows, a robber the wheel, a fisher the fishes, a fowler the birds, and a hunter the wild beasts. What other reason is there for this, save that man does not know or estimate himself or his own powers, or reflect that he is a lesser universe, and has the firmament with its powers hidden within himself?[8]

In other words, Paracelsus argues that the relation expressed by the signature is not a causal relation. Rather, it is something more complex, something which has a retroactive effect on the *signator* and which needs to be understood.

2

Before moving to the analysis of the signatures that the Archeus imprints on natural things, Paracelsus refers to the existence of a signatory art (*Kunst Signata*) that constitutes, so to speak, the paradigm of every signature. This originary signature is language, by means of which "the first *signator*," Adam, imposed on all things their "true and genuine names" (*die rechte Namen*) in Hebrew.[9]

> The signatory art teaches how to give true and genuine names to all things. All of these Adam the Protoplast truly and entirely under-stood. So it was that after the Creation he gave its own proper name to everything, to animals, trees, roots, stones, minerals, metals, waters, and the like, as well as to other fruits of the earth, of the water, of the air, and of the fire. Whatever names he imposed upon these were rati-fied and confirmed by God. Now these names were based upon a true and intimate foundation, not on mere opinion, and were derived from a predestinated knowledge, that is to say, the signatorial art. Adam is the first signator.[10]

Every name in Hebrew that left Adam's mouth had a correspon-dence in the specific nature and virtue of the named animal. "So when we say, 'This is a pig, a horse, a cow, a bear, a dog, a fox, a sheep, etc.,' the name of a pig indicates a foul and impure animal. A horse indicates a strong and patient animal; a cow, a voracious and insatiable one; a bear, a strong, victorious, and untamed animal; a fox, a crafty and cunning animal; a dog, one faithless in its nature; a sheep, one that is placid and useful, hurting no one."[11]

The relation between the signature and the signed is generally understood in terms of similarity, as in the case (to which we will turn in a moment) of the similarity between the spots in the shape of an ocellus on the *Euphrasia*'s corolla and the eyes that it has the power to heal. Since language is the archetype of the signature, the signatory art par excellence, we are obligated to understand this similarity not as something physical, but according to an analogical and immaterial model. Language, then, which preserves the archive of immaterial similarities, is also the reliquary of signatures.

3

The systematic core that determined the success of Paracelsian medicine during the Renaissance and the Baroque period concerned signatures as ciphers of the therapeutic power of plants. Signatures are, as Henry More wrote almost a century after Paracelsus' death, "natural hieroglyphics," through which God reveals medicinal virtues hidden in the vegetal world. All the more surprising is their absence in this context in *De signatura rerum*. Their place, as examples of the Archeus's signature, is taken by deer and cow horns, whose shape reveals the animal's age or the number of calves it has delivered, or the knots in the umbilical cords of newborns, which indicate how many children the mother can still have. Paracelsus's medical works, however, offer a wide array of examples. The *satyrion* is "formed like the male privy parts," and this signature shows that it can "restore a man's virility and passion."[12] The *Euphrasia*, which has a marking in the shape of an eye, thus reveals its capacity to heal the diseases of the eye.[13] If the plant called *Specula pennarum* cures women's breasts, this is because its shape recalls that of breasts. Pomegranate seeds and pine nuts, having the shape of teeth, alleviate their pain. In other cases, the similarity is metaphorical: the thistle, fraught with thorns, will alleviate sharp and acute pains; *Syderica*, whose leaves

36

have markings that look like snakes, is an antidote to every type of poisoning.

Consider the specific structure that defines signatures in this case: the signature relation, in the *Euphrasia*, is established not between, as it might seem, the hidden therapeutic virtue and the marking in the shape of an eye on the corolla but directly between the *Euphrasia* and the eyes. Paracelsus writes: "Why does the *Euphrasia* cure the eyes? Because it has in itself the *anatomiam oculorum*; it has in itself the shape and image of the eyes, and hence it becomes entirely eye."[14] The signature puts the plant in relationship with the eye, displacing it into the eye, and only in this way does it reveal its hidden virtue. The relation is not between a signifier and a signified (*signans* and *signatum*). Instead, it entails at least four terms; the figure in the plant, which Paracelsus often calls *signatum*; the part of the human body; the therapeutic virtue; and the disease — to which one has to add the *signator* as a fifth term. Signatures, which according to the theory of signs should appear as signifiers, always already slide into the position of the signified, so that *signum* and *signatum* exchange roles and seem to enter into a zone of undecidability. This sliding movement can be observed in a passage from the *Paragranum*, where Paracelsus establishes the identity between a metal — iron — and a planet (Mars), which should be its *signator*. Paracelsus writes, "What then is *ferrum*? Nothing other than Mars. What is Mars? Nothing other than *ferrum*. This means that both are *ferrum* and Mars . . . . He who knows Mars knows *ferrum* and he who knows *ferrum* knows what Mars is."[15]

4

We have left for last the discussion that holds the place of privilege in the *De signatura rerum,* namely, that of signatures whose *signator* is the human being. The example Paracelsus provides of such signatures is perhaps the most surprising in the history of the concept of signatures, even though for centuries it remained a sort of dead end in the Paracelsian episteme, before being provisionally resurrected in the thought of Foucault and Melandri. To understand natural and supernatural signatures correctly, writes Paracelsus, one needs to understand above all else those signatures whose *signator* is the human being. The first example of this is the "small yellow patch" (*ein Gelbs Flecklin*) that the Jews wear on their jackets or coats: "What is this but a sign by which anybody who meets him may understand that he is a Jew?"[16] A similar sign — the comparison here is not ironic — makes a private soldier or a bailiff (*Scherg oder Büttel*) recognizable. Just as couriers wear insignia on their garments that identify them as messengers — and also show where they come from, who sent them, and how they should be treated — so does the soldier on the battlefield wear colored signs or bands making him recognizable by friends and enemies ("Hence it is known that one is on the side of Caesar, or of the kings; that one is an Italian, another a Gaul, etc.").[17]

Still more interesting is another set of examples where the paradigm of signatures is further complicated. This group has to do with the "marks and signs" (*Markt und Zeichen*) with which the artisan marks his own works "so that everyone may understand who has produced it." Here the signature shows its likely etymological connection with the act of signing a document, which is clear in languages, like French and English, that use the word "signature" (in canon law *signaturae* were the rescripts granted by the pope by virtue of a signature on a document). However, in Latin *signare* also means "to coin," and another example discussed by Paracelsus pertains to signs that indicate the value of coins: "It should be remembered that every coin carries its proof and sign by which it may be known how much that coin is worth."[18] Like the seal impressed on a letter, these serve not to identify the sender but to signify its "force" (*Kraft*): "The seal is the confirmation of the letter which gives it authority among men and in trials. A receipt without a seal is dead, useless, empty."[19] The letters of the alphabet are also signatures made by man as *signator*: "By a few letters, names, or words, many things are designated, just as books which, though lettered outside with only one word, in that way signify their contents."[20] Or the letters inscribed on labels that in pharmacies or alchemists' laboratories allow one to recognize "liquors, syrups, oils, powders, seeds, ointments . . . spirits, oils, phlegmata, crocuses, alkalis;" or the numbers on rooms and dwellings, which mark the year in which they were built.[21]

5

Let us try to develop and analyze the unique structure of human signatures. Consider the signature (or monogram) the artisan or artist uses to mark his own work. What happens when we observe a painting in a museum and we realize that the phrase *Titianus fecit* is written in a cartouche on the lower edge? We are now so used to looking for and receiving this type of information that we do not pay attention to the operation implicit in the signature, an operation that is anything but trivial.

Let us assume that the painting represents the Annunciation, which may itself be seen both as sign and as image, harking back to a religious tradition or iconographic theme with which we are familiar (though we needn't be). What does the signature *Titianus fecit* add to the sign "Annunciation" that we have before our eyes? It tells us nothing about its theological meaning or the way in which the iconographic theme has been treated, nothing about the properties of the thing in its objective materiality. The signature merely puts the painting in relation to the name of a man, whom we know to be a famous painter who lived in Venice in the sixteenth century (but it could also be a name that we know nothing or almost nothing about). If this information were missing, the painting would remain completely unchanged in its materiality and quality. Yet the relation introduced by the signature is so important in our culture (in others, this may not be the case, and the painting could live in total anonymity) that the reading of the cartouche radically modifies how we look at the painting in question. Furthermore, if the artwork is one which falls within the era of authorial copyright, the signature has legal effects.

Now consider the example of a signature stamped on a coin which determines its value. In this case, too, the signature has no substantial relation with the small circular metal object that we hold in our hands. It adds no real properties to it at all. Yet once again, the signature decisively changes our relation to the object as well as its function in society. Just as the signature, without altering in any way the materiality of Titian's painting inscribes it in the complex network of relations of "authority," here it transforms a piece of metal into a coin, producing it as money.

And what about the letters of the alphabet which, according to Paracelsus, by being arranged into words allow us to designate books? Here it is probably not a matter of words understood as expressions of the "signatory art" that allowed Adam to assign names to the creatures. Instead, it must refer to a use of a language that is constituted not by sentences but by paradigms, initials, and conventional titles, similar to those Foucault must have had in mind when, to define his enunciative statements, he wrote that A, Z, E, R, T is, in a typing handbook, the statement of the alphabetical order adopted by French keyboards.

In all these cases, a signature does not merely express a semiotic relation between a *signans* and a *signatum*; rather, it is what — persisting in this relation without coinciding with it — displaces and moves it into another domain, thus positioning it in a new network of pragmatic and hermeneutic relations. In this sense, the yellow patch on a Jew's coat and the colored mark of the bailiff or of the courier are not merely neutral signifiers referring to the signified "Jew," "bailiff," or "courier." By shifting this relation into the pragmatic and political sphere, they express instead how one must comport oneself before Jews, bailiffs, or couriers (as well as the behavior that is expected from them). Similarly, a signature in the shape of an eye on a *Euphrasia* petal is not a sign that signifies "eye." Rather, in the eye-shaped spot (which in itself is a sign that refers back to the eye), the signature shows that the plant is an effective remedy against illnesses of the eye.

6

From the moment of its title, Jakob Böhme's *De signatura rerum* refers to Paracelsus, taking up a number of his themes and motifs—above all, the theme of Adam's language. The theory of signatures, however, is taken further here, and shows the inadequacy of the concept of the sign to address the issue. A signature, first of all, is no longer understood simply as what manifests the occult virtue of things by establishing a relation between different domains. Instead, it is the decisive operator of all knowledge, that which makes the world, mute and without reason in itself, intelligible. Böhme writes: "All whatever is spoken, written, or taught of God, without the Knowledge of the signature [*Signatur*] is dumb and void of Understanding; for it proceeds only from an historical Conjecture, from the Mouth of another, wherein the Spirit without Knowledge is dumb; but if the Spirit opens to him the *Signature*, then he understands the Speech of another; and further he understands how the spirit has manifested and revealed itself (out of the Essence through the Principle) in the Sound with the Voice."[22] For Böhme, the process of revelation, whose paradigm is language, entails from the beginning a more complex development of the semiotic model. The sign (which he calls *Bezeichnung*) itself is inert and mute, and must, in order to effect knowledge, be animated and qualified in a signature (and to describe this process, he uses the word *inqualiren*, one of the fundamental technical terms of his thought). Böhme goes on to argue: "So that in the Word may be understood in what the Spirit has conceived, either in Good or Evil; and with this sign [*Bezeichnung*] he enters into another Man's Form [*Gestaltnis*], and awakens also in the other such a form in the Signature; so that both Forms mutually assimulate together [*miteinander inqualiren*] in one Form, and then there is one Comprehension, one Will, one Spirit, and also one Understanding."[23] Even clearer is the following passage, where Böhme compares signs to a lute that remains silent as long as the player does not play it: "The signature stands in the Essence, and is as a Lute that lies still, and is indeed a dumb Thing that is neither heard or understood; but if it be played upon, then its form is understood.... Thus likewise the sign [*Bezeichnung*] of Nature in its Form is a dumb Essence.... In the human Mind, the Signature lies most artificially composed, according to the Essence of all Essences, and Man wants nothing but the wise Master that can strike his instrument."[24]

Despite the terminological hesitations, the signature here clearly does not coincide with the sign, but is what makes the sign intelligible. The instrument was prepared and marked at the moment of creation, but produces knowledge only in a subsequent moment when it reveals itself in the signature, where "the inward manifests itself in the Sound of the Word, for that is the Mind's natural Knowledge of itself."[25] Using a term that refers to a tradition that is both theological and magical, Böhme defines as "character" this active moment when signification crosses over into "revelation" (*Offenbarung*). He writes: "The whole outward visible World with all its Being is a sign [*Bezeichnung*], or Figure [*Figur*] of the inward spriritual World; whatever is internally, and however its Operation is [*in der Wirkung ist*], so likewise it has its character externally."[26]

For Böhme, the paradigm of this "natural language" (*Natursprache*) of signatures is not Paracelsus's signatory art but Christology. For him, "the Word of God is the Ground of all Substances, and the Beginning of all Properties, Qualities, or Conditions. The Word is God's speaking [*das Sprechen*], and remains in God; but the Outspeaking or Expression [*Aussprechen*], *viz.* the Exit of the Word wherein the abyssal Will introduces itself into Separability, through the Outspeaking, [is] Nature and Property."[27]

The aporias in the theory of the signature repeat those of the Trinity: just as God was able to conceive and give shape to all things by means of the Word alone, as both the model and the effective instrument of creation, the signature is what makes the mute signs of creation, in which it dwells, efficacious and expressive.

7

Before disappearing from Western science at the end of the eighteenth century, the theory of signatures exerted a decisive influence on science and magic in the age of the Renaissance and the Baroque, even to the degree of influencing non-marginal aspects of the work of Johannes Kepler and G. W. Leibniz. However, the theory of signatures did not have its locus in medical science and magic alone. Its most significant development came in the theological realm, especially in the theory of the sacraments.

The medieval hermeneutic tradition traced the inscription of the sacraments within the domain of signs back to Augustine, insofar as his was the first effort to construct the doctrine of sacraments as a "sacred semiology." Although we find in Augustine both the cursory definition of the sacrament as a *sacrum signum*

("A sacrifice as commonly understood, therefore, is the visible sacrament of an invisible sacrifice: that is, it is a sacred symbol.") and the elusively stated idea of an indelible character imprinted by the sacrament on the person who receives it, the construction of a proper theory of the sacrament as sign began only six centuries later with Berengarius of Tours and culminated in Saint Thomas's *Summa theologiae*.[28] In the passage just mentioned from *The City of God*, the term *sacramentum* refers not to the sacraments in a technical sense but more generally to "every work done in order that we may draw near to God in holy fellowship," in opposition to the sacrifice of immolation celebrated by the Hebrews, according to the biblical story.[29] Before Augustine, in Ambrose's treatise on the sacraments, the term *spiritale signaculum* only designated a moment within the process of baptism, which appears at this stage as an exorcism or initiation rite. And it is significant that in the texts where Augustine elaborates his theory of signs, which is so important for medieval theology and philosophy, he never mentions the sacraments.

The process that led to the formation of the Scholastic theory of the sacraments is usually described as the convergence or succession of three doctrines: the doctrine of the mystery sacrament (which has its paradigm in Isidore), the doctrine of the medicine sacrament (still present in Hugh of St. Victor as well as in Aquinas's *Summa contra gentiles*), and the doctrine of the sign sacrament (which supplied the definitive canonical form to the Scholastic doctrine of the sacraments). A more subtle analysis shows that the three elements continue to be present throughout all stages of the theory's development, testifying to a composite origin that has not yet been elucidated by historical investigations and that the theory of the sign sacrament is unable to get to the bottom of.

The inadequacy of the semiotic model for explaining the sacrament emerges when one tries to engage what is in every sense the most decisive problem of the theory of the sign sacrament: the question concerning the efficacy of the sign. In Hugh of St. Victor's *Sacraments of the Christian Faith*, such efficacy — together with its resemblance to the signified — grounds the difference and even the excess of the sacrament with respect to the sign. He writes: "What is the difference between sign and sacrament? The sign signifies by means of an institution [*ex institutione*]; the sacrament represents also by means of similarity [*ex similitudine*]. Furthermore, the sign may signify the thing, but not confer it [*conferre*]. In the sacrament, instead, there is not only signification but also efficacy, such that it signifies by means of institutions, represents by means of similarity, and confers by means of sanctification."[30]

The anonymous author of the *Summa sententiarum* stresses once again and without reservations the irreducibility of the sacrament to the sign:

> [The sacrament] is not only the sign of a sacred thing; it is also efficacy. This is the difference between sign and sacrament: for the sign to be, it is enough that it signify that of which it offers the sign, without conferring it. The sacrament, however, not only signifies but confers that of which it is sign or signification. In addition, there is a difference insofar as the sign exists only for signification, even if it lacks similarity, as, for example, the circle, which in the taverns signifies wine (*circulus vinum*) whereas the sacrament not only signifies by means of institution but also represents by means of similarity.[31]

8

In the treatise on the sacraments from the *Summa theologiae* which is usually seen as the moment where Aquinas fully adheres to the paradigm of the sign sacrament, the inability of the theory of the sign to fully account for the sacrament's efficacy emerges with respect to the effects of the sacrament, namely, grace and character. To explain how a sign may also be the cause of grace, Thomas is forced to distinguish between a "principal cause," which produces its effects in virtue of its form (like fire warming up in virtue of its warmth), and an "instrumental cause," which acts not in virtue of its form but only through a movement impressed on it by an acting principle (the hatchet being the cause of the bed only by means of the artisan's action). Whereas the principal cause cannot be the sign of its effect, the instrumental cause, writes Thomas, "can be called the sign of a hidden effect in virtue of the fact that it is not only a cause but in some sense an effect too, inasmuch as it receives its initial impetus from the principal agent. And this is why the sacraments of the New Law are causes and signs at the same time. Hence too it is that, as the usual formula puts it, *they effect what they figuratively express* [*efficiunt quod figurant*]."[32] However, this means that as the effect of a principal agent's action, namely Christ's, the sacrament understood as instrumental cause does not act simply *ex institutione* like a sign; rather, each time it needs an active principle in order to animate it. This is why it is necessary for the minister, who represents Christ as the principal agent, to have the intention (if not presently, at least customarily) of carrying out the sacramental act. Thomas adds:

> Thus the act of washing with water, which takes place in baptism, can be aimed at physical cleanliness or physical health, or be done in play, and there are many other reasons of this kind why this action should be performed. And because of this it is necessary to isolate and define the one purpose for which the action of washing is performed in baptism, and this is done through the intention of the minister. This intention in turn is expressed in the words pronounced in the sacraments, as when the minister says, "I baptise you in the name of the Father etc."[33]

Even if such intention is not something subjective, which

depends on the good or evil dispositions of the minister (*ex opere operantis*), but is an objective reality that is produced *ex opere operatum*, the sign here is always the place of an operation that actualizes its efficacy.

In other words, the sacrament functions not as a sign that, once instituted, always signifies its meaning but as a signature whose effect depends on a *signator*, or in any case on a principle — occult virtue in Paracelsus, instrumental virtue in Thomas — which each time animates it and makes it effective.

9

The proximity of the sign to the sphere of signatures is even more evident in the specific sacramental effect that takes the name of "character" in baptism, confirmation, and ordination (which, in contrast to the other sacraments, can be imparted only once). Augustine developed a theory of character in the context of his polemics against the Donatists, especially in the short treatise *Contra epistolam Parmeniani*. The Donatists denied the validity of baptism (and ordination) if the sacrament had been administered by or to a heretic or schismatic. For Augustine, this raised an important question because he wanted to affirm the validity of the sacrament not only independently of the situation of the subjects receiving or administering it but also outside the grace communicated by the sacrament through the Spirit. For the Donatists, the sacraments of heretics could not communicate spiritual grace, since according to the patristic tradition, they were excluded from participating in the Holy Spirit. Against this thesis, Augustine affirms the possibility of a *baptisma sine spiritu* — that is, a baptism that imprints on the soul a *character* or *nota*, without conferring its corresponding grace. The reasons for such a radical thesis are probably ecclesial, and to be found in Augustine's desire to ensure the identity of both the Christian person and the priest beyond any personal merit or unworthiness. In any case, the status of such a "character" is so paradoxical that Augustine has to multiply the paradigms in order that they may make it intelligible. He first cites the example of someone who has stamped a gold or silver coin with a *signum regale*, though illicitly, without the sovereign's authorization: if caught, he will certainly be punished, but the coin remains valid and is incorporated into the public treasury (*thesauris regalibus congeretur*).[34] The second example has to do with a soldier who, as was customary in the Roman army, has been marked on his body by the *character militiae* and out of cowardice has fled from battle. If he appeals to the emperor's clemency and is forgiven, it is not necessary to mark him again with a new *character*. "Is it possible," asks Augustine, "that the *sacramenta christiana* are less lasting than this bodily mark [*corporalis nota*]?"[35] On the basis of this example and aware of the aporias implicit in this notion, he draws by means of a doubtful argument the inevitable conclusion of a "baptism without spirit": "If baptism cannot be without the Spirit, then heretics have the Spirit—but to destruction not to salvation, just as was the case with Saul. . . . [But if] the covetous have not the Spirit of God, and yet have baptism, it is possible for baptism to exist without the Spirit of God."[36]

The idea of an indelible "sacramental character" arises, then, from the need to explain how the sacrament survives in conditions that should have made it void or inefficacious. If the communication of the Spirit is impossible, the character will express the excess of the sacrament over its effect, something like a supplement of efficacy without any content other than the pure fact of being marked. If the Christian person or priest has lost all the qualities that defined him, if he has committed some disgraceful act or even denied his faith, he still retains his Christian or priestly *character*. To put it differently: character is a zero degree signature, which expresses the event of a sign without meaning and grounds—in this event—a pure identity without content.

10

The Scholastics, who centuries later developed the theory of the "sacramental character," could not have overlooked its aporetic origin. They thus attempted to give content to the Augustinian signature by affirming that it communicates to the soul a *habitus* (this is the thesis of Alexander of Hales) or a power (*potenza*). The latter is the position of Thomas, who argues that the character, even if it does not communicate grace, nevertheless does bestow upon the soul "a certain spiritual power ordered to those things which pertain to divine worship."[37]

This, however, does not resolve all the difficulties. Thomas, too, has recourse to Augustine's military paradigm, writing that in antiquity "it was usual for soldiers on enlistment for military service to be marked with some form of physical 'character' in recognition of the fact that they were deputed for some function in the physical sphere. In the same way, therefore, when in the sacraments men are deputed for some function in the spiritual sphere pertaining to the worship of God, it naturally follows that as believers they are marked off by some form of spiritual character."[38]

Character, he argues, is an indelible sign imprinted on the soul by the sensible sign of the sacrament: "The character imprinted upon the soul has the force of a sign [*habet rationem signi*] . . . for the way in which an individual is known to have been sealed with the character of baptism is that he has been washed by water which is apparent to the senses."[39] That is, in the case of baptism, the sensible sign of the sacrament produces not only the effect of grace but also another sign that is spiritual in nature and cannot be erased.

Consider the paradoxical nature of this special signature (*quaedam signatio*) that defines character.[40] A sign produced by a sign, the character exceeds the relational nature that is proper to the sign:

With regard to the relation implied by the term "sign," there has to be some basis for this. Now the immediate basis for the relationship involved in this kind of sign, namely character, cannot be the essence of the soul. Otherwise it would belong connaturally to every soul. Hence we have to postulate some property in the soul which constitutes the basis for a relation of this kind, and this is the essence of character. Hence we shall not have to assign it to the genus of relation, as some have asserted.[41]

Character, then, is a sign that exceeds the sign, and a relation that exceeds and grounds every relation. In the efficacious sign of the sacrament, character is what marks the irreducible excess of efficacy over signification. For this reason, "character has the force of a sign in relation to the sensible sacrament by which it is imprinted, but considered in itself it has the force of a principle."[42]

The paradox of sacramental theory, which makes it akin to the theory of signatures (and which probably derives from it, even though it is legitimate to suppose for both a common magical origin), is that it presents us with something that is inseparable from the sign yet irreducible to it, a character or signature that by persisting in a sign makes it efficacious and capable of action.

In both cases, the meaning of character is purely pragmatic. Just as a coin is "imprinted with a character [*charactere . . . insignitur*] ordaining it for use in commerce, and soldiers are sealed with a character inasmuch as they are deputed to military service" (both examples also appear in Paracelsus), so are the faithful marked by the character in order to be able to perform acts of worship (*ad recipiendum vel tradendum aliis ea quae pertinent ad cultum Dei*).[43]

II

A century before Augustine, the idea that the efficacy of sacred signs and practices was independent of the condition and type of participation of the subjects involved had emerged in a work that is usually seen as the first philosophical foundation of magic and theurgy: Iamblichus's *De mysteriis*. He writes:

> For even when we are not engaged in intellection, the symbols [*syn-themata*] themselves, by themselves, perform their appropriate work, and the ineffable power of the gods, to whom these symbols relate, itself recognises the proper images [*oikeias eikonas*] of itself, not through being aroused by our thought. . . . The things which properly arouse the divine will are the actual divine symbols [*theia syn-themata*]. . . . I have labored this point at some length for this reason: that you not believe that all authority over activity [*energeias*] in the theurgic rites depends on us, or suppose that their genuine performance [*alêthes . . . ergon*] is assured by the true condition of our acts of thinking, or that they are made false by our deception.[44]

Marsilio Ficino was so convinced of the relation between these texts and the Christian tradition that when he translated *De mysteriis* into Latin, together with other Greek magical treatises and the *Corpus hermeticum*, he slightly altered the passage in question to make it accord with the doctrine of the efficacy of the sacraments. Thus not only does he place before the paragraph the title (which is missing in the original) "De virtute sacramentorum," he also translates the expression *theia synthemata*, "divine signs," as "sacramenta divina." And at the end of the passage, he adds a few lines that unequivocally refer to the Christian sacrament: "When in the course of sacrifice there are symbols and *synthemata*, that is, signs and sacraments [*signacula et sacramenta*], the priest uses material things in virtue of whose ordination he realizes the external decorum; but it is God who imprints on the sacrament its efficacious force."[45]

Both the theological doctrine of the sacramental character and the medical doctrine of signatures in all likelihood owe their origin to this kind of magical-theurgic tradition. Among the texts translated by Ficino, there is a short treatise titled *De sacrificio et magia*, attributed to Proclus, in which the basic concepts we have examined so far are clearly present. Here we find, once again, the familiar idea regarding the visible signatures of things ("the stone called 'the eye of the sky' or 'eye of the sun' contains a figure resembling the pupil of the eye from which emanates a ray") as well as the idea of efficacious likeness as the foundation of magical influences: ("The ancients, having recognized these things … by means of likeness transfer divine virtues onto the inferior world; in fact, likeness is the sufficient cause that allows individual things to be bound to one another").[46]

12

The proximity between sacraments and magic is evident enough in the practice of the baptism of images and charms as reported in a 1320 consultation of Pope John XXII. The ritual baptism of magical images, which serves to increase their efficacy, must have been a widespread enough practice in those years to worry the pontiff to the point of inducing him to submit the following question to ten theologians and canon law experts:

> Do those who baptize with water, in accordance with church rituals, images, or any other object devoid of reason for the purpose of witchcraft commit the crime of heresy and should therefore be considered heretics, or should they be judged only as having committed sorcery? And how should they be punished in either case? And what is to be done with respect to those who have received such images even tough they knew that they had been baptized? And what to do with respect to those who did not know that the images had been baptized, but, knowing the power of these sorts of images, had received them for this purpose?[47]

The pope, himself a scholar of canon law, had understood that

the juridical problem posed by such a practice touched a fundamental element of doctrine, putting in question the very nature
of the sacrament. Since sacramental efficacy immediately depends
on the *signum* and the *character* rather than on the aims and the
conditions of the subjects, the person who administers the baptism of images calls into question the essence of the sacrament and
therefore commits a crime of heresy, and not a simple crime of
sorcery. In other words, the close proximity between sacramental
and magical efficacy makes the intervention of the theologian and
the canonist necessary.

This is clear in the longer and more elaborate answer given
by the Franciscan Enrico del Carretto, bishop of Lucca. Against
those who argued that it could not be a matter of a *factum hereticale*, since magical purpose was accidental with respect to faith
in the sacrament, he argued that baptism was a consecration that
added something to the consecrated thing by way of either form
or sign. The baptism of images performed for magical purposes
therefore did not merely introduce an external aim with respect
to the sacrament but was "a form of consecration [*quedam con-
secratio*] and deputation to witchcraft, through which the thing
is affected by the act or is believed to be affected by such consecration."[48] In other words, Enrico believes in the reality of the
spell performed through the baptism of images. If the magical operation were performed on an unconsecrated image, even
if the performer believed in the demon's power and pierced the
image for this reason (*ad hoc pungit ymaginem, ut dyabolus pungat
maleficiatum*), there would be sorcery rather than heresy.[49] However, if the image has been baptized in accordance with the ritual
(*modo divino*), "the consecration of the image produces a diaboli-
cal image" where the devil effectively insinuates his power.[50] The
parallelism between the efficacy of the baptized image and that
of the sacrament consists precisely in the fact that both act by
means of a sign. Indeed, the devil is present in the image not as

a "principle of movement" (*sicut motor in mobili*) but as "something marked in the sign" (*ut signatum in signo*). Just as it occurs in the sacrament, in the magical image the devil "efficaciously institutes," through the priest, "a sign relation with respect to the spell." And, as in the sacrament, whatever the performer's belief may be, "the simple fact of consecration contains the belief, and therefore makes it a case of heresy [*factum hereticale*]."[51] Magical and sacramental operations correspond to each other term for term, and the classification of the crime as a type of heresy records this proximity.

13

Astrology is a privileged site of signatures. Indeed, the magical and medical tradition examined so far has its roots in astrology. Consider the images and figures of the decans in the Arabic treatise that was translated into Latin under the title *Picatrix* or in Abû Ma'shar's *Introductorium maius*, which so fascinated Aby Warburg when he saw them sumptuously reproduced in the frescos at Schifanoia that he did not rest until he had traced their genealogy. "In this decan," we read in the *Introductorium maius* in regard to the first decan of Aries, "a black man arises with red eyes, a man of powerful stature, courage, and greatness of mind; he wears a voluminous white garment, tied around his midriff with a cord; he is wrathful, stands erect, guards, and observes."[52] In the gloomy figure of this *vir niger*, as depicted by Francesco del Cossa in the median strip of the month of March in the hall of Palazzo Schifanoia, Warburg ultimately saw a kind of "secret companion" of his life and something like a cipher of his destiny. In *Picatrix*, both the decans and the planets have a "figure" (*forma*) of this kind. Thus, while the first decan of Aries is described there as a "man with red eyes and a large beard, wrapped in a white linen cloth, making impressive gestures while he walks," the *forma Saturni*, according to *Picatrix*, is that of "a man who has a black face and camel feet, who sits at the desk holding in his right hand a pole and in his left hand an arrow or javelin."[53]

What is the meaning of these enigmatic figures so precisely recorded in the manuscripts' illustrations? Unlike the constellations, they in no way refer to the figures that the stars seem to draw in the sky, nor do they describe any properties of the zodiacal signs to which they refer. Their function becomes clear only when we place them in the technical context of the production of charms or talismans that *Picatrix* calls *ymagines*. Whatever the matter of which they are made, the *ymagines* are neither signs nor reproductions of anything: they are operations through which the forces of celestial bodies are gathered and concentrated into a point in order to influence terrestrial bodies (*ymago nihil aliud est quam vis corporum celestium in corporibus influencium*).[54] In this role, the form or figure of the planet is defined as a *significator* or *signator*, or even "root" (*radix*), of the *ymago* that gathers and directs the virtues of the stars. In this sense, the roots are themselves operations put in the service of the efficacy of images (*iste radices erunt opus celi pro effectibus ymaginum*).[55]

Both the figure in the *ymago* and the form of the planet or decan find their meaning in this efficacious operation: they are both signatures through which the influence of the stars is realized (*iste linee significant radios quos stelle proiciunt in mundo ut in centro; et ex hoc est opus et virtus ymaginum, et hoc modo operantur*).[56] Knowledge of celestial signatures is the magician's science, in the sense that producing an *ymago* means sympathetically imagining and reproducing in a signature (which can also be a gesture or a formula) the signature of the planet in question.

This is all the more true for the so-called "signs" of the zodiac as well as for the constellations themselves. It is not properly a matter of signs (what would they be signs of?) but a matter of signatures expressing a relation of efficacious likeness between the constellation and those who are born under its sign, or more generally, between the macrocosm and the microcosm. And not only is it not a matter of signs, but it is not even a matter of anything that has ever been written down. Rather, in the sky, according to the profound image proposed by Hugo von Hofmannsthal, men learned perhaps for the first time "to read what was never written." However, this means that the signature is the place where the gesture of reading and that of writing invert their relation and enter into a zone of undecidability. Here reading becomes writing, and writing is wholly resolved into reading: "The image is called image because the forces of the spirits are conjoined here: the operation of the imagination [*cogitacio*] is included in the thing that contains the virtue of the planet."[57]

14

These observations may supply the key to understanding what is at issue in the enigmatic *Bilderatlas Mnemosyne* — to which Warburg devoted the last years of his life — as well as to grasping more appropriately the concept of *Pathosformel*. The images (in fact, photographs, which were specially developed and printed in the photo lab of the Warburg Haus) making up each of the seventy-nine plates of the atlas should not be seen (as with ordinary art books) as photographic reproductions of works or objects to which we would ultimately be referring. On the contrary, they have value *in themselves*, since they themselves are *ymagines* in *Picatrix*'s sense, in which the signature of the objects they appear to reproduce has been affixed. In other words, the *Pathosformeln* are not found in works of art or in the mind of the artist or of the historian: they coincide with the images precisely recorded in the atlas. Just as the *Introductorium maius* or *Picatrix* offers to the magician perusing its pages the catalog of the *formae* and signatures of the decans and planets that will enable him to produce

his charms, so *Mnemosyne* is the atlas of signatures that the artist — or the scholar — must learn to know and handle if he or she
wishes to understand and perform the risky operation that is at
issue in the tradition of the historical memory of the West. For
this reason, Warburg, with para-scientific terminology that is,
in truth, closer to that of magic than of science, can refer to the
Pathosformeln as "disconnected dynamograms" (*abgeschnürte Dyna-
mogramme*) that reacquire their efficacy every time they encounter the artist (or the scholar). Despite the terminological uncer-
tainties that are undoubtedly influenced by the psychology of
the time, from Friedrich Theodor Vischer to Richard Wolfgang
Semon, the *Pathosformeln*, the "engrams" and the *Bilder* Warburg
seeks to grasp are neither signs nor symbols but signatures; and
the "nameless science" he was unable to found is something like
an overcoming, an *Aufhebung* of magic by means of its own instru-
ments, an archaeology of signatures.

15

In *The Order of Things*, Michel Foucault cites Paracelsus's treatise when he situates the theory of signatures in the Renaissance
episteme. In the latter, resemblance plays a decisive role, dominating until the end of the sixteenth century the exegesis and
interpretation not only of texts but also of the relation between
man and the universe. However, a world that is supported by
the thick weave of resemblances and sympathies, analogies and
correspondences stands in need of signatures, marks that teach
us how to recognize them. "There are no resemblances without signatures. The world of similarity can only be a world of
signs," and knowledge of resemblances is based on identifying
and deciphering signatures.[58] Foucault takes note of the curious,
incessant doubling that signatures introduce into the system of
resemblances:

But what are these signs? How, amid all the aspects of the world and so many interlacing forms, does one recognize that one is faced at any given moment with a character that should give one pause because it indicates a secret and essential resemblance? What form constitutes a sign and endows it with its particular value as a sign? — Resemblance does. It signifies exactly in so far as it resembles what it is indicating (that is, a similitude). . . . But what it indicates is not the homology; for its distinct existence as a signature would then be indistinguishable from the face of which it is the sign; it is *another* resemblance, an adjacent similitude, one of another type which enables us to recognize the first, and which is revealed in its turn by a third. Every resemblance receives a signature; but this signature is no more than an intermediate form of the same resemblance. As a result, the totality of these marks, sliding over the great circle of similitudes, forms a second circle which would be an exact duplication of the first, point by point, were it not for that tiny degree of displacement which causes the sign of sympathy to reside in an analogy, that of an analogy in emulation, that of emulation in convenience, which in turn requires the mark of sympathy for its recognition. The signature and what it denotes are of exactly the same nature; it is merely that they obey a different law of distribution; the pattern from which they are cut is the same.[59]

Nevertheless, just like the authors he examines, from Paracelsus to Crollius, Foucault does not define the concept of signature, which for him resolves into resemblance; however, there is a motif in his definition of the Renaissance episteme that only needs to be elaborated to identify the proper site and function of signatures. At a certain point Foucault distinguishes semiology — the set of knowledges that allow us to recognize what is a sign and what is not — from hermeneutics, which consists of the set of knowledges that allow us to discover the meaning of signs, to "make the signs speak." The sixteenth century, he suggests, "superimposed hermeneutics and semiology in the form of simili-tude. . . . The nature of things, their coexistence, the way in which they are linked together and communicate is nothing other than their resemblance. And that resemblance is visible only in the net-work of signs that crosses the world from one end to the other."[60] Yet semiology and hermeneutics do not perfectly coincide by means of resemblance; between them there remains a gap, where knowledge is produced:

> Everything would be manifest and immediately knowable if the hermeneutics of resemblance and the semiology of signatures coin-cided without the slightest parallax. But because the similitudes that form the graphics of the world are one "cog" out of alignment with those that form its discourse, knowledge and the infinite labour it involves find here the space that is proper to them: it is their task to weave their way across this distance, pursuing an endless zigzag course from resemblance to what resembles it.[61]

Although the site and nature of signatures remain problem-atic in the passage just quoted, signatures find their own locus in the gap and disconnection between semiology and hermeneu-tics. Enzo Melandri provided an early definition of the concept of signatures in this context in a 1970 article on *The Order of Things*. Starting from the noncoincidence of semiology and hermeneutics in Foucault, he went on to define the signature as what enables the transition from the one to the other: "A *signature* is a sort of sign within the sign; it is the index that in the context of a given semiology univocally makes reference to a given interpretation. A signature adheres to the sign in the sense that it indicates, by means of the sign's making, the code with which it has to be deci-phered."[62] If for the Renaissance episteme a signature thus refers to the resemblance between the sign and its designated thing, in modern science it is no longer a character of the individual sign but of its relation with other signs. In any case, "the *type* of episteme depends on the type of signature," and this is "that character of the sign, or of the system of signs, that announces by means of its making its own relation to the designated thing."[63]

16

One of the final conclusions of Émile Benveniste's work was the idea that the transition between semiology and hermeneutics is not to be taken for granted, that between the two there is an unbridgeable gap. Consider the 1969 essay "Sémiologie de la langue." There Benveniste identifies within language "a double significance" (*une double signifiance*) that corresponds to two discrete and juxtaposed planes: on the one hand, the plane of semiotics; and on the other, that of semantics. He writes:

> The semiotic denotes the mode of significance that belongs to the linguistic sign and constitutes it as a unity.... The only question raised by the sign relates to its existence, and this question is decided with a yes or no.... It exists when it is recognized as a signifier by all the members of the linguistic community.... With the semantic, we enter into a specific mode of significance that is generated by discourse. The problems posed here are a function of language as a producer of messages. The message is not reduced to a succession of unities to be identified separately; it is not the sum of signs that produces sense. On the contrary, it is the sense, globally conceived, that is realized and divided in particular "signs," namely, words.... The semantic order is identical with the world of enunciation and the universe of discourse. It is possible to show that we are dealing with two distinct orders of concepts and two conceptual universes by pointing to the different criteria of validity that are required for the one and for the other. The semiotic (the sign) must be recognized; the semantic (discourse) must be understood."[64]

According to Benveniste, Saussure's attempt to conceive of

language solely as a system of signs is insufficient and does not allow one to explain the passage from sign to speech. The semiology of language, the interpretation of language as a system of signs, was thus "paradoxically blocked by the very instrument that allowed for its creation: the sign."[65] As Saussure had intuited in notes published after his death, if language is presupposed as a system of signs, then nothing allows us to explain how these signs are transformed into discourse: "Various concepts are present in language (that is, clothed in linguistic form) such as *beef*, *lake*, *sky*, *red*, *sad*, *five*, *to split*, *to see*. At what moment, and by virtue of what operation, what interplay between them, what conditions, do these concepts form *discourse*? The sequence of these words, however enriched it might be by the ideas it evokes, will never make any human being understand that another human being, by pronouncing it, wishes to convey something specific to him."[66]

Thus Benveniste can conclude with the forceful affirmation: "The world of the sign is, in truth, closed. From the sign to the sentence there is no transition, neither by syntagmation nor by any other means. A gap separates them."[67] In Foucault's and Melandri's terms, this amounts to saying that there is no passage from semiology to hermeneutics and that we must situate signatures precisely in the "gap" that separates them. Signs do not speak unless signatures make them speak. But this means that the theory of linguistic signification must be completed with a theory of signatures. The theory of enunciation that Benveniste develops in this same period can be considered as an attempt to construct a bridge over that gap, to render thinkable the passage between the semiotic and the semantic.

17

In the same year that Benveniste published the essay "Sémiologie de la langue," Foucault published *The Archaeology of Knowledge*.

Even though Benveniste's name does not appear in the book, and Foucault might not have known his most recent articles, a secret thread unifies the manifesto of Foucauldian epistemology and Benveniste's theses. The incomparable novelty of *The Archaeology of Knowledge* is to explicitly take as its object what Foucault calls "statements." Now, statements are not merely reducible to discourse (the semantic), since Foucault takes care to distinguish them as much from the sentence as from the proposition (the statement, he writes, is "what is left when the propositional structure has been extracted and defined," a kind of residual element of "irrelevant raw material"[68]). Nor is it possible to situate the statement entirely within the semiotic sphere, thereby reducing it to signs: "It is useless therefore to look for the statement among unitary groups of signs. The statement is neither a syntagma, nor a rule of construction, nor a canonic form of succession and permutation; it is that which enables such groups of signs to exist, and enables these rules or forms to become manifest."[69]

Hence the difficulty Foucault faces in his effort to define the "enunciative function," as well as the stubbornness with which he always insists on the heterogeneous character of statements with respect to signs and to the objects they signify:

> The statement exists therefore neither in the same way as a language (*langue*) (although it is made of signs that are definable in their individuality only within a natural or artificial linguistic system), nor in the same way as the objects presented to perception (although it is always endowed with a certain materiality, and can always be situated in accordance with spatio-temporal coordinates). . . . The statement is not the same kind of unit as the sentence, the proposition, or the speech act; it cannot be referred therefore to the same criteria; but neither is it the same kind of unit as a material object, with its limits and independence.[70]

The statement cannot be identified as a sign or structure referring to a series of logical, grammatical, or syntactical relations.
Instead, it operates in signs, phrases, and sentences at the level
of their simple existence, as a bearer of efficacy, which each time
allows us to decide whether the act of language is efficacious, if the
sentence is correct, or whether an aim is realized:

> The statement is not therefore a structure . . . it is a function of exis-
> tence that properly belongs to signs and on the basis of which one
> may then decide, through analysis or intuition, whether or not they
> "make sense," according to what rule they follow one another or are
> juxtaposed, of what they are the sign, and what sort of act is car-
> ried out by their formulation (oral or written) . . . [I]t is not in itself
> a unit, but a function that cuts across a domain of structures and
> possible unities, and which reveals them, with concrete contents,
> in time and space.[71]

To be sure, Foucault realized that it was not possible to define
the statement as one level among others of linguistic analysis and
that the archaeology he sought after did not at all delimit in language a sphere comparable to that of a disciplinary knowledge.
The whole book, with its hesitations and repetitions, its interrup-
tions and resumptions, and finally its explicit admission that it
did not aim at the constitution of a science in the proper sense,
bears witness to such difficulty. To the extent that it is always
already invested in sentences and propositions, to the extent that
it does not coincide with the signifiers or with signifieds, and
that it refers to "the very fact that they are given, and the way in
which they are given," the enunciative function is almost invisible in them and must be recognized beyond or on this side of
their designation of something or their being designated by something.[72] In other words, it is necessary to "question language, not
in the direction to which it refers, but in the dimension that gives
it."[73] To grasp this, it is less a matter of capturing the whole set of

logical or grammatical rules that order communication or establish the competence of the speaking subject than it is of pausing to reflect on the "discursive practices," that is, "a body of anonymous, historical rules, always determined in the time and space that have defined a given period, and for a given social, economic, geographical, or linguistic area, the conditions of operation of the enunciative function."[74]

The whole argument acquires clarity if we hypothesize that the statements in *The Archaeology of Knowledge* take the place that in *The Order of Things* belonged to signatures. Statements, then, are situated on the threshold between semiology and hermeneutics where signatures take place. Neither semiotic nor semantic, not yet discourse and no longer mere sign, statements, like signatures, do not institute semiotic relations or create new meanings; instead, they mark and "characterize" signs at the level of their existence, thus actualizing and displacing their efficacy. These are the signatures that signs receive from the sheer fact of existing and being used — namely, the indelible character that, in marking them as signifying something, orients and determines their interpretation and efficacy in a certain context. Like signatures on coins, like the figures of the constellations and the decans in the sky of astrology, like the eye-shaped spots on the corolla of the *Euphrasia* or the character that baptism imprints on the soul of the baptized, they have always already pragmatically decided the destiny and life of signs that neither semiology nor hermeneutics is able to exhaust.

The theory of signatures (or of statements) rectifies the abstract and fallacious idea that there are, as it were, pure and unmarked signs, that the *signans* neutrally signifies the *signatum*, univocally and once and for all. Instead, the sign signifies because it carries a signature that necessarily predetermines its interpretation and distributes its use and efficacy according to rules, practices, and precepts that it is our task to recognize. In this sense, archaeology is the science of signatures.

18

In *The Archaeology of Knowledge*, Foucault often emphasizes the purely existential character of statements. Insofar as it is not a "structure" but "a function of existence," the statement is not an object endowed with real properties. It is a pure existence, the sheer fact that a certain being — language — takes place. The statement is the signature that marks language in the pure fact of its existence (*darsi*).

An attempt to link the doctrine of signatures to ontology was made by the English philosopher Edward Herbert in the seventeenth century. It concerned the interpretation of those predicates that Scholastics called "transcendents" (*trascendentia* or *trascendentalia*) insofar as, being the most general predicates, they pertain to every being through the very fact of existing. These are: *res*, *verum*, *bonum*, *aliquid*, *unum*. Every being, owing to the sheer fact of existing, is one, true, and good. For this reason, the Scholastics said that the meaning of these predicates coincides with pure existence (*reciprocatur cum ente*), and they defined its nature with the syntagma *passiones entis*; that is, the attributes a being "suffers" or receives from the very fact of being.

Herbert's great achievement was to read these transcendent predicates (or at least one of them) as signatures. While analyzing, in *De veritate* (1633), the nature and meaning of the transcendental *bonum*, he defines it as the signature that pertains to a thing through the very fact of being: "Bonitas . . . in re est ejus signatura interior [The goodness of the thing lies in its internal signature]."[75] *Bonum* is a "passion of the being," which necessarily marks the thing and displays itself as much in its sensible appearance (the "pleasant," the "beautiful") as in intellectual knowledge (intellection as perception of the *ultima bonitatis signatura*).

Let us attempt to broaden Herbert's intuition, which throws new light on an essential chapter of first philosophy, namely, the doctrine of the transcendentals. In itself, being is the most empty and generic notion, which seems not to tolerate any determinations other than the "neither ... nor" of negative theology. Yet, if we instead posit that being, through the very fact of existing, of giving itself in an entity, receives or suffers marks or signatures that orient its comprehension toward a given sphere and a certain hermeneutics, then ontology is possible as the "discourse" of being, that is, of "the passions of being." "Quodlibet ens est unum, verum, bonum": every being presents the signature of unity (which directs it toward mathematics or the theory of singularity), of truth (which orients it toward the theory of knowledge), and of the good (which makes it communicable and desirable).

Here we touch on the special relevance of the theory of signatures for ontology. It is not only that in the syntagma *passiones entis* the objective or subjective meaning of the genitive is not clear; being and its passions coincide. Existence is a transcendental dissemination in passions, that is, in signatures. Signatures (like statements with respect to language) are then that which marks things at the level of their pure existence. *On haplôs*, "pure being," is the archi-*signator* that imprints its transcendental marks on existent entities. The Kantian principle according to which existence is not a real predicate, reveals here its true meaning: being is not "the concept of something that could be added to the concept of a thing," because in truth being is not a concept but a signature. Hence, ontology is not a determinate knowledge but the archaeology of every knowledge, which explores the signatures that pertain to beings by virtue of the very fact of existing, thus predisposing them to the interpretation of specific knowledges.

19

The theory of signatures allows us also to throw light on one of the problems that have engaged scholars of the Kabbala, namely, the relation between En-Sof (God as simple and infinite Being) and the Sephiroth (the ten "words" or attributes in which God is manifested). How can multiple attributes and determinations be admitted if God is simple, one, and infinite? If the Sephiroth are in God, God's unity and simplicity are lost; if they are outside of God, they cannot be divine at all. "You will never escape from this alternative," states the philosopher in the dialogue *The Philosopher and the Kabbalist*, written by Padua's great Kabbalist Moshe Hayyim Luzzatto: "Either the Sephiroth are in God or they are not.... How can one think something divine derived from the divine? ... 'God' signifies the one who is unique and whose existence is necessary.... So we must conceive God as one, having absolute uniqueness. How can one think God in terms of multiplicity, generation, and origin of the lights from one another? ... We know that the holy one, blessed be He, is absolutely simple and no accident can be attributed to Him."[76] The same problem appears in Christian theology (as well as in Islamic and Jewish theology) in relation to the question concerning God's attributes. It is well-known that, according to Harry A. Wolfson and Leo Strauss, the history of Western philosophy and theology from Plato to Spinoza coincides with the history of the doctrine regarding the divine attributes. And, as philosophers and theologians alike do not tire of repeating, this doctrine is intrinsically aporetic. God is the absolutely simple being, in whom not only are essence and existence indistinguishable, but not even essence and attributes, or genus and species, can be distinguished. Nevertheless, if God is the absolutely perfect being, He must somehow possess all perfections and all attributes insofar as they express perfections. Thus the field is divided between those who argue that in actuality the attributes exist in God and those who maintain with equal firmness that the attributes exist only in the minds of human beings.

Signatures interrupt this false alternative. The attributes (as the Sephiroth for the Kabbalists) are neither the essence of God nor something foreign to the essence of God: they are the signatures that, by barely brushing against the absoluteness and simplicity of the being that is solely its own existing, dispose it toward revelation and knowability.

20

The concept of signature disappears from Western science with the advent of the Enlightenment. The two lines dedicated to the term in the *Encyclopédie* amount to a mocking obituary: "Rapport ridicule des plantes entre leur figure et leurs effets. Ce système extravagant n'a que trop régné." Even more significant is its gradual reemergence under different names starting in the second half of the nineteenth century. In an essay that does not have to be described in depth here since it is so well-known, the Italian historian Carlo Ginzburg has traced a precise cartography of this reemergence, which occurs in the most disparate knowledges and techniques. Ginzburg's essay spans from Mesopotamian divination to Freud, from forensic techniques of identification to art history. It should be sufficient to recall that Ginzburg reconstructs an epistemological paradigm that he defines as "evidential" (*indiziario*) in order to distinguish it from the model of Galilean science, and that concerns "highly qualitative disciplines, in which the object is the study of individual cases, situations, and documents, precisely *because they are individual*, and for this reason get results that have an unsuppressible speculative margin."[77]

Exemplary is the case of Giovanni Morelli, who between 1874 and 1876 published under the Russian pseudonym Lermolieff (the name was an anagram, or better an actual "signature": Morelli eff., that is to say, *effinxit* or *effecit*) a series of articles that would revolutionize the techniques of attribution in painting. (We owe to Morelli, among other things, the restitution to Giorgione of the

Sleeping Venus, which until then had been exhibited in the Gemäl-degalerie of Dresden as a "copy by Sassoferrato of a lost origi-nal by Titian.") The novelty of "Morelli's method," which earned the admiration of Burckhardt and Freud and the indignation of some scholars of art, lies in the fact that instead of focusing atten-tion, as art historians had until that point, on more visible stylistic and iconographic characteristics, Morelli examined insignificant details like ear lobes, the shape of fingers and toes, and "even, *hor-ribile dictu* . . . such an unpleasant subject as fingernails."[78] Precisely where stylistic control loosens up in the execution of secondary details, the more individual and unconscious traits of the artist can abruptly emerge, traits that "escaped without his being aware of it."[79]

Following in the footsteps of Enrico Castelnuovo, an art his-torian who had worked on the question of attribution, Ginzburg compares Morelli's evidential method to the one invented more or less in the same years by Arthur Conan Doyle for his detec-tive Sherlock Holmes. In *Clues, Myths, and the Historical Method*, he writes: "The art connoisseur resembles the detective who discov-ers the perpetrator of a crime (or the artist behind a painting) on the basis of evidence that is imperceptible to most people."[80] And Holmes's almost maniacal attention to the imprint of a shoe in the mud, the ashes of a cigarette on the pavement, or indeed the curve of an ear lobe (in the story "The Adventure of the Card-board Box") undoubtedly calls to mind that of Pseudolermolieff for the marginal details in the masters' paintings.

It is well known that Morelli's writings had drawn Freud's attention years before he began to develop psychoanalysis. Edgar Wind has observed that Morelli's principle according to which the personality of the author must be found where the effort is less intense, recalls that of modern psychology, according to which it is our small unconscious gestures that betray the secret of our character. In the essay "The Moses of Michelangelo,"

Freud himself states without reservations that Morelli's method is "closely related to the technique of psycho-analysis. It, too, is accustomed to divine secret and concealed things from despised or unnoticed features, from the rubbish-heap, as it were, of our observations."[81]

The nature of the clues on which the methods of Morelli, Holmes, Freud, Alphonse Bertillon, and Francis Galton are grounded comes to light in a particular way if we view it from the perspective of the theory of signatures. The details Morelli gathers of the ways in which ear lobes or fingernails are drawn, the traces Holmes investigates in the mud or in cigarette ashes, the denials or lapses on which Freud focuses his attention, are all signatures that, by exceeding the semiotic dimension in the strict sense, allow us to put a series of details into efficacious relation with the identification or characterization of a certain individual or event.

The Cabinet des Estampes at Paris's Bibliothèque Nationale holds a series of photographs that reproduce the objects and clues gathered by the police in the garden of the accused while investigating the crimes of Henri Landru (1919). It consists of a series of small, sealed displays, similar to the frames of a painting, where pins, buttons, metal clips, bone fragments, vials containing dust, and other minutiae of this kind are classified in perfect order. What is the meaning of these small collections, which irresistibly remind us of the oneiric objects of surrealism? The captions that accompany the cases leave no doubts: like clues or traces, the fragments of objects or bodies stand in a particular relation to the crime. That is, the clue represents the exemplary case of a signature that puts an insignificant or nondescript object in effective relation to an event (in this case, a crime, in Freud's case, a traumatic event) or to subjects (the victim, the murderer, the author of a painting). The "good God" who, according to Warburg's famous motto — which Ginzburg uses as an epigraph to his essay — hides in the detail, is a *signator*.

21

An actual philosophy of the signature is contained in the two fragments Walter Benjamin dedicated to the mimetic faculty. Even
though the term itself does not appear in them, what Benjamin
calls the "mimetic element" (*das Mimetische*) or "immaterial similarity" undoubtedly refers to the sphere of signatures. The specifi-
cally human faculty of perceiving similarities, whose phylogeny he
seeks to reconstruct and whose decline in our time he documents,
precisely coincides with the ability to recognize signatures that we
have examined so far. As with Paracelsus and Böhme, the sphere
of the mimetic faculty consists not only in astrology and the corre-
spondence between microcosm and macrocosm (which Benjamin
examines at some length), but above all in language (in his corre-
spondence with Gershom Scholem, the fragments in question are
presented as a "new theory of language"). From this perspective,
language — as well as writing — appears as a sort of "archive of nonsensuous similarities, of nonsensuous correspondences,"[82] which
ground and articulate "the ties not only between what is said and
what is meant but also between what is written and what is meant,
and equally between the spoken and the written."[83] The definition developed by Benjamin in regard to the magical and mimetic
element of language perfectly coincides with the definition of the
signature offered above: "The mimetic element in language can,
like a flame, manifest itself only through a kind of bearer [*Träger*].
This bearer is the semiotic element. Thus, the nexus of meaning of
words or sentences is the bearer through which, like a flash, similarity appears. For its production by man — like its perception by
him — is in many cases, and particularly the most important, tied
to its flashing up. It flits past [*Sie huscht vorbei*]."[84]

As we have seen in regard to the relationship between signatures and signs, immaterial similarity functions in Benjamin as
an irreducible complement to the semiotic element of language

without which the transition to discourse cannot be understood. Just as with Warburg's astrological signatures, it is precisely the knowledge of the mythical and magical elements of language that enables the overcoming of magic: "In this way, language may be seen as the highest level of mimetic behavior and the most complete archive of nonsenuous similarity: a medium into which the earlier powers of mimetic production and comprehension have passed without residue, to the point where they have liquidated those of magic."[85]

22

For Benjamin, especially from the time he begins to work on the Paris arcades, history is the proper sphere of signatures. Here they appear under the names of "indices" ("secret," "historical," "temporal") or of "images" (*Bilder*), often characterized as "dialectical." "The past," reads the second thesis "On the Concept of History," "carries with it a secret index by which it is referred to redemption."[86] As fragment N3,1 of *The Arcades Project* makes clear:

> For the historical index of the images not only says that they belong to a particular time; it says, above all, that they attain to legibility only at a particular time.... Every present day is determined by the images that are synchronic with it: each "now" [*jetzt*] is the now of a particular recognizability.... It is not that what is past casts its light on what is present, or what is present its light on what is past; rather, image is that wherein what has been comes together in a flash with the now to form a constellation. In other words, image is dialectics at a standstill.[87]

The fifth thesis reaffirms, once again, the flashing and precarious character of the image in the same terms that the fragment on the mimetic faculty used in regard to nonsensuous similarity:

"The true image of the past flits by [*huscht vorbei*]. The past can be seized only as an image that flashes up at the moment of its recognizability, and is never seen again."[88]

These famous definitions of the dialectical image become clearer when restored to their proper context, namely, the theory of historical signatures. It is well-known that Benjamin's research, following the examples of the surrealists and the avant-gardes, privileges objects that because they appear to be secondary or even waste (Benjamin speaks of the "rags" of history), exhibit more forcefully a sort of signature or index that refers them to the present (the arcades, which already in the 1930s had become obsolescent and almost oneiric, are their prototype). The historical object is never given neutrally; rather, it is always accompanied by an index or signature that constitutes it as image and temporally determines and conditions its legibility. The historian does not randomly or arbitrarily choose the documents out of the inert and endless mass of the archive but follows the subtle and obscure thread of signatures that demand to be read here and now. And the status of the scholar depends, for Benjamin, precisely on the ability to read these ephemeral signatures.

23

Fashion is a privileged site of signatures. It is where signatures exhibit their genuinely historical character. For the currentness that fashion continuously seeks to recognize always constitutes itself by means of a never-ending network of references and temporal citations which define it as a "no longer" or an "again." That is to say, fashion introduces into time a peculiar discontinuity, which divides it according to its currency or outdatedness, its being or no-longer-being in fashion. This caesura, albeit subtle, is nevertheless clear insofar as those who must perceive it necessarily either perceive it or miss it, and precisely in this manner attest to their being in or out of fashion; however, if we try to objectify it or fix it in chronological time, it proves to be ungraspable.

The signature of fashion tears the years (the 1920s, the 1960s, the 1980s) out of linear chronology, allowing them to have a special relation with the designer's gesture, who cites them to make them appear in the incalculable "now" of the present. Yet this present is in itself ungraspable, since it lives only in kairological (not chronological!) relation to the signatures of the past. For this reason, being in fashion is a paradoxical condition that necessarily entails a certain ease or an imperceptible lag, in which up-to-dateness includes within itself a small part of its outside, a tinge of the démodé. Like a historian, the man of fashion is able to read the signatures of the time only if he instead of entirely placing himself in the past or coinciding wholly with the present, lingers in their "constellation," that is, in the very place of signatures.

24

Indicium (clue) and *index* derive from the Latin verb *dico*, which originally means "to show" (to show by means of the word and, therefore, to say). Linguists and philologists have long observed the essential bond that joins the lexical family of *dico* to the sphere of law. "To show by words" is the proper operation of the juridical formula, the uttering of which realizes the condition necessary to produce a certain effect. Thus, for Benveniste, the term *dix*—which survives only in the phrase *dicis causa* ("for form's sake")—means "the fact of showing verbally and with authority what must be."[89] *Index* is "the one who shows or indicates by means of the word," just as *iudex* is "the one who says the law." To the same group belongs the term *vindex*, which denotes the one who in a trial takes the place of the accused and declares himself ready to suffer the consequences of the proceedings.

Pierre Noailles has clarified the meaning of this last term. It is derived, according to the traditional etymology, from *vim dicere*: literally, "to say or to show force." But what kind of "force" is involved here? Among the scholars, observes Noailles, the greatest confusion prevails on this point:

> They incessantly oscillate between the two possible meanings of the word: force or violence, that is, force that is materially put in action. In actuality, they do not choose, but rather each time propose either one or the other meaning. The *vindicationes* of the *sacramentum* are presented at one time as manifestations of force, and at another as acts of symbolic or simulated violence. The confusion is even greater in regard to the *vindex*. In fact, it is not clear whether the force or violence expressed is his own, which he puts at the service of the law, or the violence of the adversary whom he denounces as contrary to justice.[90]

Against such confusion, Noailles shows that the *vis* in question cannot be a force or a material violence but must instead be only the force of ritual, namely, a "force that compels, but does not need to apply itself materially in an act of violence, albeit a simulated one."[91] On this point, Noailles cites a passage from Aulus Gellius in which the "vis civilis...quae verbo diceretur" (civil force...which is said by means of words) is placed in opposition to the "vis quae manu fieret, cum vi bellica et cruenta." If we further develop Noailles's thesis, it is possible to offer the hypothesis that "the force said by means of the word" in question in the action of the *vindex* is the force of the efficacious formula, as the originary force of the law. That is to say, the sphere of law is that of an efficacious word, a "saying" that is always *indicere* (proclamation, solemn declaration), *ius dicere* (saying what is in conformity with the law), and *vim dicere* (saying the efficacious word). If this is true, then law is the sphere of signatures par excellence, where the efficacy of the word is in excess of its meaning (or realizes it). At the same time, the whole of language here shows its originary belonging to the sphere of signatures. Before (or better, together with) being the place of signification, language is the place of signatures, without which no sign would be able to function. And speech acts, in which language seems to border on magic, are only the most visible relics of this archaic signatory nature of language.

25

All research in the human sciences — particularly in a historical context — necessarily has to do with signatures. So for the scholar it is all the more important to learn to recognize and handle them correctly, since in the final analysis they determine the success of any scholar's investigation. Gilles Deleuze once wrote that a philosophical inquiry entails at least two elements: the identification of the problem and the choice of concepts that are adequate for approaching it. It is necessary to add that concepts entail signatures, without which they remain inert and unproductive. It may even happen that what at first appears to be a concept is later revealed to be a signature (or vice versa). Thus, we have seen that in first philosophy the transcendentals are not concepts but signatures and "passions" of the concept of "being."

In the human sciences, too, we may at times deal with concepts that in actuality are signatures. One such concept is secularization, about which in the mid-1960s in Germany there was a sharp debate that involved figures like Hans Blumenberg, Karl Löwith, and Carl Schmitt. The discussion was vitiated by the fact that none of the participants seemed to realize that "secularization" was not a concept, in which the "structural identity" between theological and political conceptuality (Schmitt's thesis) or the discontinuity between Christian theology and modernity (this was Blumenberg's thesis *contra* Löwith) was in question. Rather, secularization was a strategic operator that marked political concepts in order to make them refer to their theological origins. To put it differently: secularization acts within the conceptual system of modernity as a signature, which refers it back to theology. Just as, according to canon law, the priest reduced to a secular status had to bear a sign of the order to which he had belonged, so the "secularized" concept shows its past in the theological sphere as a signature. Secularization, then, is a signature that marks or exceeds a sign or concept in order to refer it to a specific interpretation or to a specific sphere without, however, leaving it in order to constitute a new concept or new meaning. What is really at stake in the (ultimately political) debate that has engaged scholars from Max Weber's time to the present can be understood only if we grasp the signatory character of secularization.

What is decisive each time is the way we understand the reference worked by the signature. Many of the doctrines that have dominated the debate in twentieth-century philosophy as well as the human sciences entail a more or less conscious practice of signatures. Indeed, it would not be wrong to state that the basis of one important part of twentieth-century thought presupposes something like the absolutizing of the signature, that is to say, a doctrine of the constitutive primacy of signatures over signification.

Consider the concept of privative opposition in Nikolai Trubetzkoy, which has exerted a determinant influence on the human sciences of the twentieth century. It implies that the non-marked term is not opposed to the marked term as an absence is to a presence, but rather that non-presence is somehow equivalent to a zero degree of presence (that presence is *lacking* in its absence). In the same sense, according to Roman Jakobson, the zero sign or phoneme, though not having any differential character, functions precisely to oppose itself to the simple absence of the phoneme. The philosophical foundation of these concepts lies in Aristotle's theory of "privation" (*sterêsis*), of which Hegel's concept of *Auf-hebung* is the consistent development. Indeed, according to Aristotle, privation is distinguished from simple "absence" (*apousia*) insofar as it still entails a referral to the form of which it is a privation, which is somehow attested through its own lack.[92]

At the end of the 1950s, Claude Lévi-Strauss elaborated these concepts in his theory of the constitutive excess of the signifier over the signified. According to Lévi-Strauss, signification is originally in excess over the signifieds that are able to fill it, and this gap translates into the existence of free or floating signifiers that are in themselves devoid of meaning. In other words, it is a matter of non-signs or signs having *"zero symbolic value*, that is, a sign marking the necessity of a supplementary symbolic content."[93] This theory becomes clear when read as a doctrine of the constitutive priority of the signature over the sign. The zero degree is not a sign but a signature that, in the absence of a signified, continues to operate as the exigency of an infinite signification that cannot be exhausted by any signified.

Once again, everything depends on the way in which we understand this primacy of signatures over the sign. The ephemeral success of deconstruction in the last thirty years of the twentieth century was intimately tied to an interpretative practice that suspends signatures and makes them idle, in such a way that there is never any access to the realized event of meaning. In other words, deconstruction is a way of thinking about signatures as pure writing beyond every concept, which thus guarantees the inexhaustibility—the infinite deferral—of signification. This is the sense of the notions of "archi-trace" and "originary supplement" as well as the insistence with which Derrida affirms the nonconceptual character of these "undecidables": it is a matter not of concepts but of archi-signatures or "signatures at degree zero," which are always already posited as supplement with respect to every concept and every presence. A signature, separated at the origin and from the origin in the position of supplement, exceeds every meaning in a ceaseless *différance* and erases its own trace in a pure auto-signification. "Therefore the sign of this excess must be absolutely excessive as concerns all possible presence-absence... and yet, *in some manner* it must still signify.... The trace is produced as its own erasure."[94] A signature's auto-signification never grasps itself, nor does it let its own insignificance be; rather, it is displaced and deferred in its own gesture. The trace is then a signature suspended and referred toward itself, a *kenôsis* that never knows its own *plêrôma*.

The strategy of Foucault's archaeology is entirely different. It, too, starts with the signature and its excess over signification. However, just as there is never a pure sign without signature, neither is it possible ever to separate and move the signature to an originary position (even as supplement). The archive of signatures that in *The Archaeology of Knowledge* gathers the non-semantic mass that is inscribed into every signifying discourse and surrounds and limits the acts of speech as an obscure and insignificant margin, also defines the whole set of rules that determine the conditions of the existence and operation of signs, how they make sense and are juxtaposed to one another, how they succeed one another in space and time. Foucauldian archaeology never seeks the origin or its absence. As the 1971 essay "Nietzsche, Genealogy, History" never tires of repeating, to produce a genealogy of knowledge or of morals does not mean to seek its origin, ignoring as irrelevant or inaccessible the details and accidents that accompany every beginning, or the episodes and accidents of its history. On the contrary, it means keeping events in their own proper dispersal, lingering on the smallest deviations and the aberrations that accompany them and determine their meaning. In a word, it means seeking in every event the signature that characterizes and specifies it and in every signature the event and the sign that carry and condition it. To put it in Foucault's words:

79

"to show that to speak is to do something — something other than to express what one thinks."[95]

It goes without saying that deconstruction and archaeology do not exhaust the catalog of signatorial strategies. It is possible, for example, to imagine a practice that without infinitely dwelling in pure signatures or simply inquiring into their vital relations with signs and events of discourse reaches back beyond the split between signature and sign and between the semiotic and the semantic in order to lead signatures to their historical fulfillment. Whether a philosophical inquiry is possible that reaches beyond signatures toward the Non-marked that, according to Paracelsus, coincides with the paradisiacal state and final perfection is, as they say, another story, for others to write.

CHAPTER THREE

Philosophical Archaeology

I

The idea of a "philosophical archaeology" appears for the first time in Kant. In his "jottings" for the essay "What Real Progress Has Metaphysics Made in Germany Since the Time of Leibniz and Wolff," Kant explores the possibility of a "philosophizing history of philosophy." A philosophical history of philosophy, he writes, "is itself possible, not historically or empirically, but rationally, i.e., *a priori*. For although it establishes facts of reason, it does not borrow them from historical narrative, but draws them from the nature of human reason, as philosophical archaeology [*als philoso-phische Archäologie*]." The paradox implicit in such an archaeology is that, since it cannot merely be a history of what philosophers have "been able to reason out concerning the origin, the goal, and the end of things in the world," that is, of "opinions [*Meynungen*] that have chanced to arise here or there," it runs the risk of lacking a beginning and putting forth a "history of the thing that has not happened."[1]

Kant's notes return more than once to this paradox: "One cannot write a history of the thing that has not happened, and for which nothing has ever been provided as preparation and raw materials."[2] He adds: "All historical knowledge is empirical.... Thus a historical presentation of philosophy recounts how philosophizing has been done hitherto, and in what order. But philosophizing is a gradual development of human reason, and this cannot have set forth, or even have begun, upon the empirical path, and that by mere concepts."[3] Finally: "A history of philosophy is of such a special kind, that nothing can be told therein of what has happened, without knowing beforehand what should have happened, and also what can happen."[4]

Let us pause on the rather peculiar character of this science that Kant calls "philosophical archaeology." This science appears as a "history," and as such it cannot but question its own origin; however, since it is a, so to speak, a priori history, whose object coincides with the very end of humanity, that is, the development and exercise of reason, the *archê* it seeks can never be identified with a chronological datum; it can never be "archaic." Furthermore, since philosophy is concerned not only with what has been but also with what ought to or could have been, it ends up being in a certain sense something that has not yet been given, just as its history is "the history of the thing that has not happened."

For this reason, Kant argues in the *Logic* that "every philosophical thinker builds his own work, so to speak, on the ruins [*auf den Trümmern*] of another," and that "one cannot learn philosophy, because *it is not yet given*."[5] Archaeology, then, is a science of ruins, a "ruinology" whose object, though not constituting a transcendental principle in the proper sense, can never truly be given as an empirically present whole. The *archai* are what could or ought to have been given and perhaps one day might be; for the moment, though, they exist only in the condition of partial objects or ruins. Like philosophers, who do not exist in reality, they are given only as *Urbilder*, archetypes or original images.[6] An "archetype," adds Kant, "remains such only if it can never be reached. It must serve only as a guideline [*Richtschnur*]."[7]

2

The idea that every authentic historical practice contains an essential dishomogeneity, a constitutive gap between the *archê* it investigates and factical origin, is at the basis of Foucault's 1971 essay "Nietzsche, Genealogy, History." The essay's strategy is immediately clear: it is a matter of playing genealogy, whose model Foucault reconstructs from Nietzsche, against any search for an origin. From this perspective, it may even be useful to seek an alliance with history: "Genealogy does not oppose itself to history . . . on the contrary, it rejects the metahistorical deployment of ideal significations and indefinite teleologies. It opposes itself to the search for 'origins.'"[8] Thus, among the terms employed by Nietzsche, Foucault distinguishes *Ursprung*, which he reserves for "origin," the *bête noir* from which we must stay away, and the two terms that "are more exact than *Ursprung* in recording the true object of genealogy": *Herkunft*, which he translates as "descent," and *Entstehung*, "emergence, the moment of arising."[9] If Nietzsche refutes the pursuit of the origin it is because *Ursprung* names "the exact essence of things, their purest possibilities, and their carefully protected identities; because this search assumes the existence of immobile forms that precede the external world of accident and succession. This search is directed to 'that which was already there,' the 'very same' of an image of a primordial truth fully adequate to its nature, and it necessitates the removal of every mask to ultimately disclose an original identity."[10]

Genealogy goes to war against this idea. It is not that the genealogist does not look for something like a beginning. However, what he or she finds "at the historical beginning of things" is never the "inviolable identity of their origin." Thus "a genealogy of values, morality, asceticism, and knowledge will never confuse itself with a quest for their 'origins,' will never neglect as inaccessible all the episodes of history. On the contrary, it will cultivate the details and accidents that accompany every beginning. . . . The genealogist needs history to dispel the chimeras of the origin."[11] The French term *conjurer*—translated here as dispel—encompasses two opposite meanings: "to evoke" and "to expel." Or perhaps these two meanings are not opposites, for dispelling something — a specter, a demon, a danger — first requires conjuring it. The fact is that the alliance between the genealogist and the historian finds its meaning precisely in this "evocation-expulsion." Years later, in a 1977 interview, the same gesture will define the relation between genealogy and the subject: one has to account for the constitution of the subject within the weavings of history to get rid of it once and for all: "It is necessary to get rid of the subject itself by getting rid of the constituting subject, that is, to arrrive at an analysis that would account for the constitution of the subject in the historical plot. This is what I would call genealogy: to account for the constitution of knowledge, discourses, spheres of objects, etc. without having to refer to a subject."[12]

The operation involved in genealogy consists in conjuring up and eliminating the origin and the subject. But what comes to take their place? It is indeed always a matter of following the threads back to something like the moment when knowledge, discourses, and spheres of objects are constituted. Yet this "constitution" takes place, so to speak, in the non-place of the origin. Where then are "descent" (*Herkunft*) and "the moment of arising" or "emergence" (*Entstehung*) located, if they are not and can never be in the position of the origin?

3

The idea that all historical inquiry involves the identification of a fringe or of a heterogeneous stratum that is not placed in the position of a chronological origin but is qualitatively other, derives not from Nietzsche but from Franz Overbeck, the theologian who was perhaps the most faithful and lucid of Nietzsche's friends. Overbeck calls "prehistory" (*Urgeschichte*) this dimension with which every historical inquiry — and not just Church history — must necessarily engage. Thus he writes: "It is only when starting from the essential difference between prehistory and history that one can explain why prehistory enjoys such a special consideration. Prehistory is in fact — and absolutely — more relevant and more decisive than any history, even outside of the history of the Church. The history of the moment of arising or emergence [*Entstehungsgeschichte*] is of incomparable value for the history of every living being and, more generally, of life."[13]

For Overbeck, this means that every historical phenomenon necessarily splits itself into prehistory and history (*Urgeschichte* and *Geschichte*), which are connected but not homogeneous, and therefore require different methodologies and precautions. Prehistory does not merely coincide chronologically with what is most ancient:

> The fundamental character of prehistory is that it is the history of the moment of arising [*Entstehungsgeschichte*], and not, as its name might lead one to believe, that it is the most ancient [*uralt*]. Indeed, it may even be the most recent, and the fact of being recent or ancient in no way constitutes a quality that belongs to it in an original way. Such a quality is as difficult to perceive in it as any relation to time that belongs to history in general. Instead, the relation to time that belongs to history is attributed to the subjectivity of the observer. Like history in general, prehistory is not tied to any specific site in time.[14]

At first glance, the heterogeneous character of prehistory has an objective foundation insofar as "history begins only where the monuments become intelligible and where trustworthy written testimonies are available. Behind and on this side of it, there lies prehistory." Nevertheless, the following passage clarifies beyond all doubt that at issue is not an objective given, but rather a constitutive heterogeneity inherent in historical inquiry itself, which each time must confront a past of a, so to speak, special type: "prehistory, too, has to do with the past, but with the past in a special sense," with respect to which "the veil that is suspended over every tradition darkens to the point of impenetrability."[15] In his essay, *Über die Anfänge der patristischen Literatur*, Overbeck distinguishes a *christliche Urliteratur* and an *urchristliche Literatur*; and in a posthumous work he makes clear that "the past of an *Urliteratur* is not a simple past, but a qualified past or a past to the second power — more-than-past [*Mehr-als-Vergangenheit*] or superpast [*Übervergangenheit*]: there is nothing or almost nothing of the past in it."[16]

History and prehistory, originally unified, irrevocably separate from each other at a certain point:

> In the history of every organism, there comes the moment when the limits dividing it from the world can no longer be *shifted*. In that instant, prehistory or the history of the moment of arising [*Entstehungsgeschichte*] separates itself from history. Hence the similarity between this moment and death and the ease with which every history—understood in the common sense of the term—appears as a history of decline [*Verfallsgeschichte*]. It loosens once again the bond among elements that prehistory has produced.... Therefore, if one has to distinguish, within the things that have a life and historical efficacy, between their prehistorical and historical epochs, it is prehistory that lays out the foundation of their historical efficacy.[17]

It is not only that prehistory and history are distinct, albeit connected. The very historical efficacy of a phenomenon is bound up with this distinction.

In fact, in prehistory, the elements that in history we are used to considering as separate coincide immediately and manifest themselves only in their living unity. Take the case of a book. In prehistory, argues Overbeck, it

> acts as a closed unity of itself and the author.... At this time, to take a book seriously means knowing of its author nothing else beyond the book. The historical efficacy of the book is grounded on such a

unity, though it dissolves in the course of its effectivity, until in the end the book lives by itself, and no longer its author in it. This is the time of literary history, whose fundamental motif is the reflection on the author of books that are now the only things left alive.... At this stage, the book...acts separately from its author, though a process is thereby introduced that in the end will exhaust every efficacy.[18]

4

Anyone who practices historical inquiry must sooner or later engage the constitutive heterogeneity inherent in his or her work. This can be done in the form of either the critique of tradition or the critique of sources, both of which demand special care. Criticism concerns not just the ancient character of the past but above all the mode in which the past has been constructed into a tradition. Overbeck, having long worked on the patristic sources, is perfectly aware of this:

> There is no history without tradition—but if every history is thus accompanied by a tradition, this does not mean...that what is called tradition is always the same thing.... The writer of history must approach its exposition by means of a tireless preliminary work: this is the critique of tradition. To the extent that historiography presupposes this critique and that criticism's claims to autonomy are justified, then the necessity of retracing every period back to its tradition is established and it is right to ask if the tradition of prehistory should not be described before the tradition of every other period.[19]

The critique of tradition (and of sources as well) deals not with a meta-historical beginning but with the very structure of historical inquiry. It is along these lines that one should reread the pages of section 6 of *Being and Time* which Heidegger dedicates to the "destruction of tradition" and where it is possible to perceive echoes of Overbeck's thought. The famous distinction between "history" (*Historie*) and "historicality" (*Geschichtlichkeit*) elaborated there is not metaphysical, nor does it simply imply an opposition between object and subject. The distinction becomes intelligible as soon as it is referred to its context, namely, the distinction between tradition and source criticism. Heidegger writes:

> When tradition thus becomes master, it does so in such a way that what it "transmits" is made so inaccessible, proximally and for the most part, that it rather becomes concealed. Tradition takes what has come down to us and delivers it over to self-evidence; it blocks our access to those primordial "sources" from which the categories and concepts handed down to us have been in part genuinely drawn. Indeed it makes us forget that they have had such an origin, and makes us suppose that the necessity of going back to these sources is something which we need not even understand.[20]

The "destruction of tradition" must confront this freezing of tradition in order to enable "the return to the past" (*Rückgang zur Vergangenheit*), which coincides with renewed access to the sources.

Overbeck calls "canonization" the mechanism by which tradition bars access to the sources, which is especially true in regard to the original Christian literature.[21] To be sure, there are also other ways in which access to the sources is barred or controlled. In modern culture, one of these occurs when knowledge defines and regulates textual criticism, thereby transforming the very access to the sources into a special tradition, namely, the study of the manuscript tradition. If philology performs a necessary and healthy critique of such tradition, it cannot ipso facto give back to the critical text that it produces its character as a source; it cannot constitute it as a moment of arising. And in those cases where it is possible to go back not so far as the archetype but to the autograph, the access to the source character of a text — that is, its prehistory — requires a further operation. The source, understood as the moment of arising, does not coincide with the documents of the manuscript tradition, even though clearly it is not possible to gain access to the source without undertaking a firsthand analysis of that tradition. The inverse, furthermore, is not true: it is possible to access the manuscript tradition without having access to the source as moment of arising (anyone familiar with current philological practice knows that this, in fact, is the rule, whereas going back from the manuscript tradition to the *Urgeschichte* — which entails the capacity to renew knowledge of that tradition — is the exception).

But what does the scholar seek to return to when engaging in a critique of tradition and the canon? Clearly the problem here is not merely philological, because even the necessary philological precautions for such inquiry are complicated when dealing with *Urgeschichte* and *Entstehung*. It is not possible to gain access in a new way, beyond tradition, to the sources without putting in question the very historical subject who is supposed to gain access to them. What is in question, then, is the epistemological paradigm of inquiry itself.

Provisionally, we may call "archaeology" that practice which in any historical investigation has to do not with origins but with the moment of a phenomenon's arising and must therefore engage anew the sources and tradition. It cannot confront tradition without deconstructing the paradigms, techniques, and practices through which tradition regulates the forms of transmission, conditions access to sources, and in the final analysis determines the very status of the knowing subject. The moment of arising is objective and subjective at the same time and is indeed situated on a threshold of undecidability between object and subject. It is never the emergence of the fact without at the same time being the emergence of the knowing subject itself: the operation on the origin is at the same time an operation on the subject.

5

An important precaution must be taken whenever one presupposes a unitary (or in any case, more originary) prehistoric stage before a historical split with which we are familiar. For example, consider the division between the religious and the profane juridical spheres, each of whose distinctive characteristics appear to be well-defined, at least to a certain extent. If a more archaic stage is reached in one of these spheres, we are often led to hypothesize that there was a previous stage beyond it in which the sacred and the profane spheres were not yet distinct. Hence Louis Gernet, whose work concerns the most ancient Greek law, has called "pre-law" (*pré-droit*) an originary phase in which law and religion were indiscernible. And Paolo Prodi, in his inquiry on the political history of the oath, similarly evokes a "primordial instinct" in which the process of separation between religion and politics had not yet begun.[22] In such cases, one must take care not merely to project upon the presupposed "primordial instinct" the characteristics defining the religious and political spheres known to us, which are precisely the outcome of the split. Just as a chemical compound has specific properties that cannot be reduced to the sum of its elements, what stands prior to the historical division is not necessarily the sum of the characteristics defining its fragments. Prelaw (conceding that such a hypothesis could make sense) cannot simply be a more archaic law, just as what stands before religion as we historically know it is not just a more primitive religion. Rather, one should avoid the very terms "religion" and "law," and try instead to imagine an *x* that we must take every care in defining, practicing a kind of archaeological *epochê* that suspends, at least provisionally, the attribution of predicates that we commonly ascribe to religion and law. In this sense, too, prehistory is not homogeneous with history and the moment of arising is not identical with what comes to be through it.

6

In the 1973 introduction to the third volume of *Mythe et épopée*, Georges Dumézil sought to define his own research methods, which he resolutely described as "historical," in a polemic against the structuralism prevalent at the time.

> I am not a structuralist; I do not have the opportunity to be or not to be one. My effort is that not of a philosopher but of a historian, a historian of the oldest history and fringe of ultra-history [*de la plus vieille histoire et de la frange d'ultra-histoire*] that one can reasonably attempt to reach; this is limited to the observation of primary data in spheres that are known to be genetically akin and then, through the comparison of some of these primary data, going back to the secondary data that constitute their common prototypes.[23]

As Dumézil readily acknowledges, this method is derived from the comparative grammar of Indo-European languages: "What is sometimes called 'Dumézil's theory' consists entirely in remembering that at a certain point Indo-Europeans existed and to think, following in the linguists' footsteps, that the comparison of the most ancient traditions of peoples who are at least in part their heirs must allow us to catch a glimpse of the basic outlines of their ideology."[24]

The consistency of the "fringe of ultra-history" that the historian attempts to reach here is therefore intimately tied to the existence of the Indo-European language and of the people who spoke it. It exists in the same sense and in the same measure in which an Indo-European form exists (for example, *deiwos* or *med*, forms that are usually preceded by an asterisk so that they can be distinguished from the words belonging to the historical languages). However, rigorously speaking, each of these forms is nothing but an algorithm that expresses a system of correspondences between existing forms in the historical languages, and, in Antoine Meillet's words, what we call Indo-European is nothing but "a system of correspondences . . . that presupposes a language *x* spoken by people *x* at place *x* and at time *x*," where *x* merely stands for "unknown."[25]

Unless one wants to legitimze the *monstrum* of a historical inquiry that produces its original documents one can never extrapolate from the Indo-European language events supposed to have taken place historically. This is why Dumézil's method made a significant advance on the comparative mythology of the end of the nineteenth century, when, around 1950, he recognized that the ideology of the three functions (priests, warriors, shepherds, or, in modern terminology, religion, war, and economy) "did not necessarily translate, in the life of a society, into an *actual* tripartite division of this society, based on the Indian model [of the three castes]," but rather represented more of an ideology, something like "an ideal and, at the same time, a way of analyzing and interpreting the forces that determined the course of the world and the life of men."[26]

The "oldest history," the "fringe of ultra-history," that archaeology seeks to reach cannot be localized within chronology, in a remote past, nor can it be localized beyond this within a meta-historical atemporal structure (for example, as Dumézil said ironically, in the neuronal system of a hominid). Like Indo-European words, it represents a present and operative tendency within historical languages, which conditions and makes intelligible their development in time. It is an *archê*, but, as for Foucault and Nietzsche, it is an *archê* that is not pushed diachronically into the past, but assures the synchronic comprehensibility and coherence of the system.

7

The term "archaeology" is linked to Michel Foucault's investigations. It had made its discreet — though decisive — first

appearance in the preface to *The Order of Things*. There archaeology, in contrast to history in the "traditional meaning of that
word," is presented as an inquiry into an at once transcendental
and paradigmatic dimension, a sort of "historical a priori," where
knowledge finds its condition of possibility. This dimension is "the
epistemological field, the *episteme* in which knowledge, envisaged
apart from all criteria having reference to its rational value or
its objective forms, grounds its positivity and thereby manifests
a history which is not that of its growing perfection, but rather
that of its conditions of possibility."[27] Foucault specifies that it is
not so much a history of ideas or of sciences as it is an inquiry
that, by going back upstream in the history of discursive formations, knowledge, and practices seeks to discover "on what basis
knowledge and theory became possible; within what space of
order knowledge was constituted; on the basis of what historical
a priori, and in the element of what positivity, ideas could appear,
sciences be established, experience be reflected in philosophies,
rationalities be formed, only, perhaps, to dissolve and vanish
soon afterwards."[28]

Let us pause on the oxymoron "historical a priori." As in
the 1971 essay, it aims to underscore that it is not a matter of a
meta-historical origin, a kind of originary gift that founds and
determines knowledge. As Foucault made clear three years later
in *The Archaeology of Knowledge*, the episteme is itself a historical practice, "a total set of relations that unite, at a given period,
the discursive practices that give rise to epistemological figures, sciences, and possibly formalized systems."[29] The a priori
that conditions the possibility of knowledge is its own history
grasped at a specific level. This is the ontological level of its
simple existence, the "brute fact" of its existing at a particular
time and in a certain way; or, to use the terminology from the
Nietzsche essay, the brute fact of its "moment of arising" (or,
in Overbeck's terms, its prehistory). Yet how can an a priori

be given and exist historically? And how is it possible to gain access to it?

In all probability, the idea of a "historical a priori" originates more from Marcel Mauss than from Kant's philosophical archaeology. In his *General Theory of Magic* (1902–1903), Mauss argues that *mana* is "the very condition of magical experimentation" and "exists, *a priori*, before all other experience. Properly speaking, it is not a magical representation in the same way as those representations of sympathy, demons, and magical properties. It produces magical representations and is a condition of them. It functions as a kind of category, making magical ideas possible in the same way as we have categories which make human ideas possible." With a significant elaboration, Mauss defines this historical transcendental as "an unconscious category of understanding," implicitly suggesting in this way that the epistemological model required for such knowledge cannot be entirely homogeneous with that of conscious historical knowledge.[30] But as with Foucault, it is nevertheless clear that for Mauss the a priori, though conditioning historical experience, is itself inscribed within a determinate historical constellation. In other words, it realizes the paradox of an a priori condition that is inscribed within a history and that can only constitute itself a posteriori with respect to this history in which inquiry — in Foucault's case, archaeology — must discover it.

8

Foucault did not question the specific temporal structure that seems to be implied by the notion of a historical a priori. Yet the past in question here is, like Overbeck's prehistory and Dumézil's "fringe of ultra-history," a special kind of past that neither precedes the present chronologically as origin nor is simply exterior to it (in this sense, in Overbeck's words, it contains "nothing or almost nothing of the past"). In his essay on déjà vu, Henri Bergson put forth the thesis that memory does not follow perception, but rather is contemporaneous with it, and can thus, as soon as the attention of consciousness relaxes, produce a "false recognition" that he defines with the only apparently paradoxical expression "a memory of the present." Such a memory, he writes, "is of the past in its form and of the present in its matter."[31] Moreover, if perception corresponds to the actual and the image of memory to the virtual, then the virtual will, for Bergson, necessarily be contemporaneous with the real.

In the same sense, the condition of possibility in question in the historical a priori that archaeology seeks to reach is not only contemporaneous with the real and the present. It is and remains immanent in them as well. With a singular gesture, the archaeologist pursuing such an a priori retreats, so to speak, toward the present. It is as if, considered from the viewpoint of archaeology or its moment of arising, every historical phenomenon split in accordance with the fault line separating in it a before and an after, a prehistory and a history, a history of the sources and a historical tradition that are in actuality contemporaneous, insofar as they coincide for an instant in the moment of arising.

Walter Benjamin must have had something similar in mind when, following in Overbeck's footsteps, he wrote that in the monadological structure of the historical object are contained both its "prehistory" and its "post-history" (*Vor- und Nachgeschichte*), or when he suggested that the entire past must be brought into the present in a "historical apocatastasis."[32] (For Origen, *apokatastasis* is the restitution of the origin that will take place at the end of time; by characterizing an eschatological reality as "historical," Benjamin makes use of an image quite similar to Foucault's "historical a priori.")

9

Enzo Melandri deserves credit for grasping early on the philosophical relevance of Foucault's archaeology and for seeking to
develop and clarify its structure. Melandri notes that while usually the basic codes and matrices of a culture are explicated by a
recourse to a code of a higher order to which a mysterious explica-
tive power is attributed (this is the model of the "origin"), with
Foucault "archaeological inquiry instead sets out to overturn the
procedure or better to make the explication of the phenomenon
immanent in its description."[33] This entails a sharp refutation of
metalanguage and instead assumes a "paradigmatic matrix, both
concrete and transcendental, that has the function of giving form,
rule, and norm to a content" (this is the model of the "historical a priori").[34] Melandri seeks to analyze this immanent matrix
by locating it vis-à-vis the Freudian opposition between the conscious and the unconscious.

Paul Ricoeur had already spoken of an "archaeology of the subject" in regard to the primacy of the past and the archaic in Freud's
thought. Freudian analysis shows that the secondary process of
consciousness is always delayed with respect to the primary process of desire and the unconscious. The wish fulfillment pursued
by the dream is necessarily regressive insofar as it is modeled on
the "indestructible desire" of an infantile scene, whose place it
takes. For this reason, writes Ricoeur: "Regression, of which
dreams are the witness and the model, shows that man is unable
to completely and definitively effect this replacement except in
the inadequate form of repression; repression is the ordinary
rule or working condition of a psychism condemned to making a late appearance and to being ever prey to the infantile, the
indestructible."[35] Ricoeur argues that next to this archaeology in
the strict sense of the word, there is in Freud's metapsychologi-
cal writings a "generalized archaeology" as well, which concerns

the psychoanalytic interpretation of culture: "The genius of Freudianism is to have unmasked the strategy of the pleasure principle, the archaic form of the human, under its rationalizations, its idealizations, its sublimations. Here the function of the analysis is to reduce apparent novelty by showing that it is actually a revival of the old: substitute satisfaction, restoration of the lost archaic object, derivatives from early fantasies — these are but various names to designate the restoration of the old in the features of the new."[36]

Melandri's conception of archaeology is entirely different. Just as for Foucault, the point of departure lies in Nietzsche — in particular, the concept of a "critical history" from the second essay in *Untimely Meditations*, that is to say, a history that criticizes and destroys the past to make life possible.[37] Melandri renders this concept more general by connecting it, through an extraordinary tour de force, to Freud's concept of regression:

> [Critical history] must retrace in the opposite direction the actual genealogy of events that it examines. The division that has been established between historiography (*historia rerum gestarum*) and actual history (*res gestae*) is quite similar to the one that, for Freud, has always existed between the conscious and the unconscious. Critical history thus has the role of a therapy aimed at the recovery of the unconscious, understood as the historical "repressed." Ricoeur and Foucault, as just mentioned, call this procedure "archaeological." It consists in tracking genealogy back to where the phenomenon in question splits into the conscious and the unconscious. Only if one succeeds in reaching that point does the pathological syndrome reveal its real meaning. So it is a matter of a *regression*: not to the unconscious as such, but to what made it unconscious — in the dynamic sense of repression.[38]

While the link between archaeology and regression was already established in Ricoeur, Melandri radically inverts its sign in this dense passage. The pessimistic vision of regression, which is incapable of overcoming the original infantile scene, cedes its place to an almost soteriological vision of an archaeology capable of going back, regressively, to the source of the split between conscious and unconscious. But how are we to understand this singular "archaeological regression," which does not seek to reach the unconscious or the forgotten in the past so much as to go back to the point where the dichotomy between conscious and unconscious, historiography and history (and, more generally, between all the binary oppositions defining the logic of our culture), was produced? It is not merely a question of bringing the repressed, which comes back in the form of a symptom, to consciousness, as the vulgate of the analytic model would have it. Nor is it a matter of writing the history of the excluded and defeated, which would be completely homogeneous with the history of the victors, as the common and tedious paradigm of the history of the subaltern classes would have it. Melandri makes clear that archaeology is to be understood precisely as a regression and as such it is the opposite of rationalization. He writes:

> For archaeology, the concept of regression is essential. Furthermore, the regressive operation is the exact reciprocal of rationalization. Rationalization and regression are inverse operations, just like the differential and the integral.... To take up a very well-known expression of Nietzsche's, which has nevertheless not yet been understood (and if what we are saying is true, then it is also true that it will unfortunately never be possible to understand it entirely), we may say at this point that archaeology requires a "Dionysian" regression. As Valéry observes, *nous entrons dans l'avenir à reculons*.... To understand the past, we should equally traverse it *à reculons*.[39]

10

The image of a procession in time that turns its back on the goal is, of course, found as well in Benjamin, who must have been familiar with Valéry's citation. In the ninth thesis, the angel of history, whose wings are caught in the storm of progress, advances toward the future *à reculons*. Melandri's "Dionysian" regression is the inverse and complementary image of Benjamin's angel. If the latter advances toward the future with a gaze fixed on the past, Melandri's angel regresses into the past while looking at the future. Both proceed toward something that they can neither see nor know. The invisible goal of these two images of the historical process is the present. It appears at the point where their gazes encounter each other, when a future reached in the past and a past reached in the future for an instant coincide.

What happens when archaeological regression reaches the point where the split between conscious and unconscious, between historiography and history that defines the condition in which we find ourselves is produced? It should by now be obvious that our way of representing the moment before the split is governed by the split itself. To imagine such a "before" indeed involves, following the logic inherent in the split, presupposing an original condition prior to it that at a certain point divided itself. In this case, this is expressed by the tendency to represent the before or the beyond of the dichotomy as a state of happiness, a kind of golden age devoid of repressions and perfectly conscious of and master of itself. Or, as in Freud and Ricoeur, as the infinite repetition of the infantile scene, the indestructible manifestation of the phantasm of desire. On the contrary, before or beyond the split, in the disappearance of the categories governing its representation, there is nothing but the sudden, dazzling disclosure of the moment of arising, the revelation of the present as something that we were not able to live or think.

II

The idea that the present might be given in the form of a constitutive inaccessibility is bound up with Freud's conception of
trauma and repression. According to this conception, an actual
experience — a train crash, an infantile scene (generally concerning sexuality), a drive — is repressed into the unconscious
either because of its traumatic character or because it is for
some reason unacceptable for consciousness. It thus enters a
stage of latency during which it seems as if it had, so to speak,
never taken place. Yet during this stage neurotic symptoms
or oneiric content begin to appear in the subject, bearing witness to the return of the repressed. Thus Freud writes: "What
a child has experienced and not understood by the time he has
reached the age of two he may never again remember, except
in his dreams. . . . At any time in later years, however, [those
events] may break into his life with obsessive impulsiveness,
direct his actions, force him to like or dislike people, and often
decide the choice of his love-object by a preference that so
often cannot be rationally defended."[40] Only analysis is able to
go beyond the symptoms and compulsive actions, back to the
repressed events.

In *Moses and Monotheism*, Freud applies this scheme to the
history of the Jews. The imposition of the law by Moses was followed by a long period in which the Mosaic religion entered a
stage of latency, only to appear later in the form of the Judaic
monotheism with which we are familiar. Freud institutes in
light of this a parallelism between the "special state of memory
that . . . we class as 'unconscious'" and historical tradition. Thus
he writes: "In this feature we expect to find an analogy with
the state of mind that we ascribe to tradition when it is active
in the mental emotional life of a people."[41] In other words, with
respect to its *traditum*, tradition functions as a period of latency
in which the traumatic event is preserved and at the same

time repressed (according to the etymology that unites *tradere* and *tradire*).

In her book *Unclaimed Experience*, Cathy Caruth suggests that latency is somehow constitutive of historical experience and that the traumatic event is preserved and experienced precisely and only through its forgetting:

> The experience of trauma, the fact of latency, would thus seem to consist not in the forgetting of a reality that can hence never be fully known, but in an inherent latency within the experience itself. The historical power of the trauma is not just that the experience is repeated after its forgetting, but that it is first experienced at all.... For history to be a history of trauma means that it is referential precisely to the extent that it is not fully perceived as it occurs; or to put it somewhat differently, that a history can be grasped only in the very inaccessibility of its occurrence.[42]

Let us try to elaborate these ideas, which the author leaves unexplained, with reference to archaeology. They imply above all that not only memory, as in Bergson, but also forgetfulness, are contemporaneous with perception and the present. While we perceive something, we simultaneously remember and forget it. Every present thus contains a part of non-lived experience. Indeed, it is, at the limit, what remains non-lived in every life, that which, for its traumatic character or its excessive proximity remains unexperienced in every experience (or, if you wish, in the terms of Heidegger's history of being, it is what in the form of forgetting destines itself to a tradition and to a history). This means that it is above all the unexperienced, rather than just the experienced, that gives shape and consistency to the fabric of psychic personality and historical tradition and ensures their continuity and consistency. And it does so in the form of the phantasms, desires, and obsessive drives that ceaselessly push at the threshold of consciousness (whether individual or collective). To paraphrase a saying of

Nietzsche's, one might say that whoever (an individual or a people) has not experienced something always has the same experience.

12

The analogy between archaeological regression and psychoanalysis now seems clearer. In both cases, it is a question of gaining access to a past that has not been lived through, and therefore that technically cannot be defined as "past," but that somehow has remained present. In the Freudian scheme, such a non-past bears witness to its having been by means of neurotic symptoms, which are used in analysis as an Ariadne's thread to go back to the originary event. In genealogical inquiry, the access to the past that has been covered over and repressed by tradition is made possible by the patient work that rather than searching for the origin, focuses on the moment of arising. Yet how is it possible to gain access, once again, to a non-lived experience, to return to an event that somehow for the subject has not yet truly been given? Archaeological regression, going back to the hither side of the dividing line between the conscious and the unconscious, also reaches the fault line where memory and forgetting, lived and non-lived experience both communicate with and separate from each other.

It is not, however, a matter of realizing, as in the dream, the "indestructible desire" of an infantile scene, nor, as in the pessimistic vision of *Beyond the Pleasure Principle*, of infinitely repeating an original trauma. Nor, as in a successful analytical therapy, of bringing back to consciousness all the content that had been repressed in the unconscious. On the contrary, it is a matter of conjuring up its phantasm, through meticulous genealogical inquiry, in order to work on it, deconstruct it, and detail it to the point where it gradually erodes, losing its originary status. In other words, archaeological regression is elusive: it does not seek, as in Freud, to restore a previous stage, but to decompose, displace, and ultimately bypass it in order to go back not to its content but to the modalities, circumstances, and moments in which the split, by means of repression, constituted it as origin. Thus it is the exact reciprocal face of the eternal return: it does not will to repeat the past in order to consent to what has been, transforming the "so it was" into "so I willed it to be." On the contrary, it wills to let it go, to free itself from it, in order to gain access beyond or on this side of the past to what has never been, to what was never willed.

Only at this point is the unlived past revealed for what it was: contemporary with the present. It thus becomes accessible for the first time, exhibiting itself as a "source." For this reason, contemporaneity, co-presence to one's own present, insofar as it entails the experience of an unlived and the memory of a forgetting, is rare and difficult; for this reason, archaeology, going back to this side of memory and forgetting, constitutes the only path of access to the present.

13

The text where Foucault perhaps most precisely described — or foresaw — the strategies and gestures of archaeology is the first essay he published, the long 1954 preface to *Le Rêve et l'existence* by Ludwig Binswanger. Even though the term itself is obviously absent, "the movement of freedom" that Foucault attributes to the dream and imagination shares the meanings and aims of archaeology. From the beginning, he refutes Freud's thesis of the dream as vicarious fulfillment of an original wish. If the dream is dream, rather than satisfied desire, this is because it "also fulfills counter-desires that are opposed to desire itself. The oneiric fire is the burning satisfaction of sexual desire, though what makes it possible for desire to take shape in the subtle substance of fire is everything that denies such desire and incessantly seeks to extinguish it." Hence, the insufficiency of Freudian analysis: the language of the dream is reduced solely to its "semantic function," leaving aside its "morphological and syntactical structure," that is to say, the fact that it articulates itself in images. For this reason, insofar as the analysis of the properly imaginary dimension of expression is entirely omitted, "psychoanalysis has never succeeded in making images speak."[43]

The movement of the dream can never exhaust itself in the restoration of an original scene or trauma because it goes well beyond them in order to reach back to the "first movements of freedom," until it coincides with the "trajectory of existence itself." For the subject, to follow such a trajectory in the dream means to put itself radically in question, above all taking the risk of its own "derealization."

> To imagine Pierre after one year of absence does not mean announcing him in the mode of unreality.... It means first of all that I derealize myself, absenting myself from this world where for me it is not possible to encounter Pierre. This does not mean that I "escape to another world," or that I walk along the possible margins of the real world. I ascend to the streets of the world of my presence; and then the lines of this necessity from which Pierre is excluded become blurred, and my presence, as presence to this world, is erased.[44]

Far from restoring a previous archaic stage, a phantasm, or a family history, the dream begins by destroying and shattering every real world while dragging itself as well into such destruction. If it goes back in time, it is in order to leap over the subjective and objective universes corresponding to it toward "the world on the daybreak of its first explosion, when it still coincided with its own existence."[45] Just as archaeology in the 1969 book is defined precisely by grasping phenomena at the level of their moment of arising and pure being-there, so in the dream "there occurs the transition from anthropology to ontology," where "existence itself . . . in the fundamental direction of the imaginary indicates its own ontological foundation."[46] And while for Freud the phantasm represents the indestructible goal orienting the movement of regression, the dream and the imagination continually call into question every crystallization of their impetus in an image or phantasm. Indeed, a phantasm is generated "when the subject finds the free movement of its existence annihilated in the presence of a quasi-perception that surrounds and immobilizes it."[47] On the contrary, "the value of a poetic imagination is measured by the power of destruction internal to the image."[48] Thus "all imagination, in order to be authentic, must learn to dream; and 'poetic art' has meaning only insofar as it teaches itself to break the spell of images in order to open to the imagination the free path toward the dream, which offers, as absolute truth, its 'indestructible kernel of night'." This dimension beyond images and phantasms toward which the movement of the imagination is directed is not the obsessive repetition of a trauma or of a primal scene, but the initial moment of existence when "the originary constitution of the world is accomplished."[49]

14

Let us elaborate the specific temporal structure implicit in a philosophical archaeology. What is at stake in it is not properly a past but a moment of arising; however, access to such can only be obtained by returning back to the point where it was covered over and neutralized by tradition (in Melandri's terms, to the point where the split occurred between the conscious and the unconscious, historiography and history). The moment of arising, the *archê* of archaeology is what will take place, what will become accessible and present, only when archaeological inquiry has completed its operation. It therefore has the form of a past in the future, that is, a *future anterior*.

Here it is not merely a matter, as has been suggested, of "an appeal for the alternative developments that had been condemned in the first trial" nor of conjecturing possible alternatives to the actual state of things.[50] Benjamin once wrote that "in remembrance we have an experience that forbids us to conceive of history as fundamentally atheological," because memory somehow modifies the past, transforming the unrealized into realized and the realized into unrealized.[51] If memory thus constitutes the force that gives possibility back to what has been (and nevertheless confirms it as past), forgetting is what incessantly removes it (and yet somehow guards its presence). Instead, the point of archaeology is to gain access to the present for the first time, beyond memory and forgetting or, rather, at the threshold of their indifference.

Precisely for this reason, the space opening up here toward the past is projected into the future. In the introduction to *Le Rêve et l'existence*, Foucault observes (contrary to Freud) the intimate tension of the dream toward the future: "The essential point of the dream is not so much that it resuscitates the past as that it announces the future. It foretells and announces the moment in which the patient will finally reveal to the analyst the secret [he or she] does not yet know, which is nevertheless the heaviest burden of [his or her] present.... The dream anticipates the moment of freedom. It constitutes a harbinger of history, before being the compelled repetition of the traumatic past."[52]

Leaving aside the accent placed here, perhaps too ingenuously, on the future as the "first moment of freedom that frees itself," we must specify that the future at issue in archaeology becomes intertwined with a past; it is a future anterior. It is the *past that will have been* when the archaeologist's gesture (or the power of the imaginary) *has cleared away* the ghosts of the unconscious and the tight-knit fabric of tradition which block access to history. Only in the form of this "will have been" can historical consciousness truly become possible.

15

Archaeology moves backward through the course of history, just as the imagination moves back through individual biography. Both represent a regressive force that, unlike traumatic neurosis, does not retreat toward an indestructible origin but rather toward the point where history (whether individual or collective) becomes accessible for the first time, in accordance with the temporality of the future anterior.

In this way, the relation between archaeology and history becomes transparent. It corresponds to the relation that in Islamic theology (and, though in a different way, in Christian and Jewish theology, too) at once distinguishes and joins redemption and creation, the "imperative" (*amr*) and "creation" (*khalq*), prophets and angels. According to this doctrine, there are two kinds of work or praxis in God: the work of redemption and that of creation. To the former correspond the prophets, who serve as mediators in order to affirm the work of salvation; to the latter correspond the angels, who mediate the work of creation. The work of salvation precedes in rank that of creation, hence the superiority of the prophets over the angels. (In Christian theology, the two works, united in God, are assigned to two distinct persons within the Trinity: the Father and the Son, the all-powerful Creator and the Redeemer, in whom God emptied himself of his force.)

The decisive aspect of this conception is that redemption precedes creation in rank, that the event that seems to follow is in truth anterior. It is not a remedy for the fall of creatures, but rather that which makes creation comprehensible, that which gives it its meaning. For this reason, in Islam, the light of the

Prophet is the first of all beings (just as in the Jewish tradition the name of the Messiah was created before the creation of the world, and in Christianity the Son, though he was generated by the Father, is consubstantial and coeval with Him). It is instructive that in Islam and Judaism the work of salvation, while preceding in rank the work of creation, is entrusted to a creature. This confirms the paradox, which should by now be familiar to us, that the two works are not simply separate but rather persist in a single place, where the work of salvation acts as a kind of a priori that is immanent in the work of creation and makes it possible.

To go backward through the course of history, as the archaeologist does, amounts to going back through the work of creation in order to give it back to the salvation from which it originates. Similarly, Benjamin made redemption a fully historical category, one opposed in every sense to the apologia of bad historians. And not only is archaeology the immanent a priori of historiography, but the gesture of the archaeologist constitutes the paradigm of every true human action. For it is not merely the work of an author's — or of anyone's — life that determines his or her rank, but the way in which he or she has been able to bring it back to the work of redemption, to mark it with the signature of salvation and to render it intelligible. Only for those who will have known how to save it, will creation be possible.

16

Before entering a stage of decline, the history of the human sciences saw, during the first half of the twentieth century, a decisive acceleration, with linguistics and comparative grammar assuming the roles of "pilot science" in the field. The idea that it might be possible, through a purely linguistic analysis, to return to more archaic stages (or ultra-historical stages, to once again take up Dumézil's expression) of the history of humanity had been put forth by Hermann Usener at the end of the nineteenth century in his work *Götternamen* (1896). At the outset of his investigation, he asked himself how the creation of divine names had been possible, and observed that in order to attempt to find an answer to such a question — one that is absolutely fundamental for the history of religions — we have no other "evidence" (*Urkunde*) than that originating from an analysis of language.[53] However, even before him, though with much less rigor, comparative grammar had inspired the investigations of scholars ranging from Max Müller to Adalbert Kuhn and Émile Burnouf, all of whom had attempted to provide a foundation for comparative mythology and the science of religions in the last thirty years of the nineteenth century. But just when comparative grammar, in its effort to reconstruct not only the "divine names" but the general outline of "Indo-European institutions" themselves through the analysis of purely linguistic data, was reaching its apex (with the publication of Benveniste's *Indo-European Language and Society*), the project started to decline in conjunction with linguistics' turn toward a formalized model à la Chomsky, whose epistemological horizon made such an endeavor inadmissible.

This is not the place to ask about the function and future of the human sciences today. Instead, we are interested once again in how the *archê* that is in question in archaeology is to be understood. If it is indeed true that inquiry had made a significant advance when it abandoned, in the fields of linguistics and the history of cultures, the anchorage in a language that was supposed to be real and in the people who spoke it ("the academic Indo-European language spoken, so one thought, 'at the moment of the dispersion'"[54]), and if scholars had understood that it was not as important to reconstruct an unverifiable prototype as it was to explain comparatively the known languages, nonetheless it was not possible within that perspective to completely cut off all the links to the ontological support implicit in the hypothesis. Thus, when in 1969 Benveniste published his masterpiece, it was by no means clear how the epistemological *locus* and historical consistency of something like an "Indo-European institution" was to be understood. And it is quite probable that Benveniste would not have been able to suggest a solution in this regard, even if he had not been struck by a type of total and incurable aphasia.

From the perspective of the philosophical archaeology proposed here, the question regarding ontological anchoring must be completely revised. The *archê* toward which archaeology regresses is not to be understood in any way as a given locatable in a chronology (even with as large a frame as prehistory); instead, it is an operative force within history, like the Indo-European words expressing a system of connections between historically accessible languages, or the child of psychoanalysis exerting an active force within the psychic life of the adult, or the big bang, which is supposed to have given rise to the universe but which continues to send toward us its fossil radiation. Yet unlike the big bang, which astrophysicists claim to be able to date (albeit in terms of million of years), the *archê* is not a given or a substance, but a field of bipolar historical currents stretched between anthropogenesis and history, between the moment of arising and becoming, between an archi-past and the present. And as with anthropogenesis, which is supposed to have taken place but which cannot be hypostatized in a chronological event — the *archê* alone is able to guarantee the intelligibility of historical phenomena, "saving" them archaeologically in a future anterior in the understanding not of an unverifiable origin but of its finite and untotalizable history.

At this point, it is also possible to understand what is at stake in the paradigm shift in the human sciences from comparative grammar (an essentially historical discipline) to generative grammar (ultimately, a biological discipline). In both cases, there remains the problem of the ultimate ontological anchoring, which for comparative grammar (and for the disciplines grounded in it) is an originary historical event and for generative grammar (and for the cognitive disciplines associated with it) is the neuronal system and genetic code of *Homo sapiens*. The current predominance in the human sciences of models originating from the cognitive sciences bears witness to this shift of epistemological paradigm. Yet the human sciences will be capable of reaching their decisive epistemological threshold only after they have rethought, from the bottom up, the very idea of an ontological anchoring, and thereby envisaged being as a field of essentially historical tensions.

Notes

CHAPTER ONE: WHAT IS A PARADIGM?

1. Michel Foucault, *The Politics of Truth*, trans. Lysa Hochroth and Catherine Porter (Los Angeles: Semiotexte, 2007), pp. 60–61.

2. Hubert Dreyfus and Paul Rabinow, *Michel Foucault: Beyond Structuralism and Hermeneutics. With an Afterword by and Interview with Michel Foucault* (Chicago: University of Chicago Press, 1983), p. 199.

3. Michel Foucault, *The Order of Things* (New York: Vintage Books, 1973), pp. 239–40.

4. Michel Foucault, introduction to *The Normal and the Pathological*, by Georges Canguilhem, trans. Caroline R. Fawcett (1978; New York: Zone Books, 1991), p. 16.

5. Thomas S. Kuhn, *The Structure of Scientific Revolutions* (Chicago: University of Chicago Press, 1970), p. 182.

6. *Ibid.*, p. 46.

7. *Ibid.*, p. 187.

8. Michel Foucault, *Dits et écrits*, ed. Daniel Defer and François Ewald (Paris: Gallimard, 1994), vol. 2, p. 240.

9. Michel Foucault, "Truth and Power," in *Power: Essential Works of Foucault 1954–1984*, ed. James D. Faubion, trans. Robert Hurley (New York: New Press, 2000), vol. 3, p. 114.

10. *Ibid.*, pp. 114–15.

11. Michel Foucault, *The Archaeology of Knowledge*, trans. A. M. Sheridan Smith (New York: Pantheon Books, 1972), p. 181.

12. *Ibid.*, pp. 186–87.

13. *Ibid.*, p. 191.

14. *Ibid.*, p. 192.

15. Michel Foucault, *Discipline and Punish: the Birth of the Prison*, trans. Alan Sheridan (New York: Vintage Books, 1995), p. 200.

16. *Ibid.*, pp. 205, 220, 221.

17. Daniel S. Milo, *Trahir le temps: Histoire* (Paris: Les Belles Lettres, 1991), p. 236.

18. Aristotle, *Prior Analytics* 69a13–15.

19. Immanuel Kant, *Critique of the Power of Judgment*, trans. Paul Guyer (Cambridge, UK: Cambridge University Press, 2000), p. 121.

20. Plato, *The Statesman* 278c.

21. Victor Goldschmidt, *Le paradigme dans la dialectique platonicienne* (Paris: Vrin, 1985), p. 53.

22. *Ibid.*, p. 77.

23. Plato, *The Statesman* 278b–c.

24. Goldschmidt, *Le paradigme dans la dialectique platonicienne*, p. 84.

25. Plato, *Republic* 6.509d–511e.

26. *Ibid.*, 6.511b2–c1.

27. *Ibid.*, 6.510b9.

28. *Ibid.*, 7.533c6.

29. Martin Heidegger, *Being and Time*, trans. John Macquarrie and Edward Robinson (New York: Harper and Row, 2008), p. 195.

30. *Ibid.*

31. Johann Wolfgang von Goethe, *Naturwissenschaftliche Schriften*, vol. 2, in *Gedenkausgabe der Werke, Briefe, und Gespräche*, ed. Ernst Beutler (Zurich: Artemis, 1949–52), vol. 17, p. 691.

32. Johann Wolfgang von Goethe, *Naturwissenschaftliche Schriften*, vol. 1, in *ibid.*, vol. 16, pp. 851–52.

33. *Ibid.*, p. 852.

34. Goethe, *Naturwissenschaftliche Schriften*, vol. 2, in *ibid.*, p. 706.

35. *Ibid.*, vol. 1, p. 871.

36. Johann Wolfgang von Goethe, *Maximen und Reflexionen*, in *ibid.*, vol. 2, p. 693.

CHAPTER TWO: THEORY OF SIGNATURES

1. Paracelsus, "Concerning the Signature of Natural Things," in *The Hermetic and Alchemical Writings: Vol. 1*, ed. Arthur Edward Waite (London: James Elliott, 1894).

2. Paracelsus, *Von den naturlichen Dingen*, in *Bücher und Schriften*, ed. Johannes Huser (1859; Hildesheim-New York: Georg Olms, 1972), vol. 3.7, p. 131.

3. Paracelsus, *Liber de podagricis*, in *ibid.*, vol. 2.4, p. 259.

4. Paracelsus, *Von den naturlichen Dingen*, in *ibid.*, vol. 3.7, p. 133.

5. Paracelsus, "Concerning the Signature of Natural Things," p. 171.

6. *Ibid.*, p. 173.

7. *Ibid.*

8. *Ibid.*, p. 174.

9. *Ibid.*, p. 188.

10. *Ibid.*

11. *Ibid.*, p. 189.

12. Paracelsus, *Selected Writings*, trans. Norbert Guterman (Princeton, NJ: Princeton University Press, 1988), pp. 122–23.

13. Paracelsus, *Bücher und Schriften*, vol. 1.2, p. 234.

14. *Ibid.*, vol. 2.4, p. 316.

15. *Ibid.*, vol. 1.2, p. 110.

16. Paracelsus, "Concerning the Signature of Natural Things," p. 172.

17. *Ibid.*

18. *Ibid.*

19. *Ibid.*

20. *Ibid.*

21. *Ibid.*

22. Jakob Böhme, *Works of Jacob Behmen: The Teutonic Philosopher: Vol. 4* (Whitefish, MT: Kessinger, 2003), p. 9.

23. Böhme, *Works of Jacob Behmen*, p. 9.

24. *Ibid.*, p. 10

25. *Ibid.*

26. *Ibid.*, p. 59.

27. *Ibid.*, p. 239.

28. Augustine, *The City of God against the Pagans*, ed. and trans. R.W. Dyson (Cambridge, UK: Cambridge University Press, 2007), p. 397.

29. *Ibid.*, p. 399.

30. Hugh of St. Victor, *De sacramentis christianae fidei*, PL, 176, p. 35a.

31. Anonymous, *Summa sententiarum*, PL, 176, p. 117b.

32. Thomas Aquinas, *Summa theologiae*, trans. David Bourke (London: Blackfriars, 1975), vol. 56, p. 55.

33. *Ibid.*, p. 127.

34. Augustine, *Contra epistolam Parmeniani*, PL, 43, p. 71.

35. *Ibid.*

36. Augustine, *On Baptism, Against the Donatists*, 5.24, trans. J. R. King, rev. Chester D. Hartranft, in *A Select Library of the Nicene and Post-Nicene Fathers of the Christian Church, Vol. 4*, ed. Philip Schaff (Buffalo, NY: Christian Literature Company, 1887), p. 475.

37. Aquinas, *Summa theologiae*, p. 83.

38. *Ibid.*

39. *Ibid.*, p. 79.

40. *Ibid.*

41. *Ibid.*, p. 83.

42. *Ibid.*, pp. 83–85.

43. *Ibid.*, p. 87.

44. Iamblichus, *De mysteriis*, trans. Emma C. Clarke, John M. Dillon, and Jackson P. Hershbell (Atlanta: Society of Biblical Literature, 2003), p. 115.

45. *Iamblichus de mysteriis Aegyptiorum, Chaldaeorum, Assyriorum; Proclus... de sacrificio et magia ... Marsilio Ficino florentino interprete* (Venice: Aldi, 1516), p. 7.

46. *Ibid.*, p. 35.

47. Alain Boureau, *Le pape et les sorciers: Une consultation de Jean XXII sur la magie en 1320* (manuscript B.A.V. Borghese 348) (Rome: École Française de Rome, 2004), p. ix.

48. *Ibid.*, p. 15.

49. *Ibid.*, p. 29.

50. *Ibid.*, p. 28.

51. *Ibid.*

52. Aby Warburg, *The Renewal of Pagan Antiquity*, trans. David Britt (Los Angeles: Getty Research Institute, 1999), p. 569.

53. David Pingree, ed., *Picatrix: The Latin Version of the Gayat al-hakim* (London: Warburg Institute, University of London, 1986), pp. 33 and 51.

54. *Ibid.*, p. 51.

55. *Ibid.*, pp. 8–9.

56. *Ibid.*, p. 8.

57. *Ibid.*, p. 111.

58. Michel Foucault, *The Order of Things* (New York: Vintage Books, 1966), p. 26.

59. *Ibid.*, pp. 28–29.

60. *Ibid.*, p. 29.

61. *Ibid.*, p. 30.

62. Enzo Melandri, "Michel Foucault: L'epistemologia delle scienze umane," *Lingua e stile* 2.1 (1967), p. 147.

63. *Ibid.*, p. 148.

64. Émile Benveniste, *Problèmes de linguistique générale* (Paris: Gallimard, 1974), vol. 2, p. 64.

65. *Ibid.*, pp. 65–66.

66. Jean Starobinski, *Words upon Words*, trans. Olivia Emmet (New Haven, CT: Yale University Press, 1979), pp. 3–4.

67. Benveniste, *Problèmes de linguistique générale*, p. 65.

68. Foucault, *The Archaeology of Knowledge*, trans. A. M. Sheridan Smith (New York: Pantheon Books, 1970), p. 84.

69. *Ibid.*, p. 88.

70. *Ibid.*, p. 86.

71. *Ibid.*, pp. 86–87.

72. *Ibid.*, p. 111.

73. *Ibid.*

74. *Ibid.*, p. 117.

75. Edward Herbert, *De veritate*, trans. Meyrick H. Carré (Bristol: J. W. Arrowsmith, 1937), p. 191.

76. Moshe Hayyim Luzzatto, *Le philosophe et le cabaliste: Exposition d'un débat*, ed. Joelle Hansel (Lagrasse: Verdier, 1991), pp. 86–87.

77. Carlo Ginzburg, *Clues, Myths, and the Historical Method*, trans. John and Anne C. Tedeschi (Baltimore: Johns Hopkins University Press, 1989), p. 106.

78. *Ibid.*, p. 101.

79. *Ibid.*

80. *Ibid.*, pp. 97–98.

81. Sigmund Freud, "The Moses of Michelangelo," in *The Standard Edition of the Complete Psychological Works of Sigmund Freud*, trans. James Strachey (London: Hogarth Press, 1953), vol. 13, p. 222.

82. Walter Benjamin, "On the Mimetic Faculty," in *Selected Writings: Volume 2, 1927–1934*, trans. Rodney Livingstone (Cambridge, MA: Belknap Press, 1999), p. 722.

83. *Ibid.*

84. *Ibid.*

85. *Ibid.*

86. Walter Benjamin, "On the Concept of History," in *Selected Writings: Volume 4, 1938–1940*, trans. Edmund Jephcott (Cambridge, MA: Belknap Press, 2003), p. 390.

87. Walter Benjamin, *The Arcades Project*, trans. Howard Eiland and Kevin McLaughlin (Cambridge, MA: Belknap Press, 1982), pp. 462–63.

88. Benjamin, "On the Concept of History," pp. 390–91.

89. Émile Benveniste, *Indo-European Language and Society*, trans. Elizabeth Palmer (Coral Gables, FL: University of Miami Press, 1973), p. 336.

90. Pierre Noailles, *Fas et jus: Études de droit romain* (Paris: Les Belles Lettres, 1948), p. 57.

91. *Ibid.*, p. 59.

92. Aristotle, *Metaphysics* 1004a.16.

93. Claude Lévi-Straus, *Introduction to the Work of Marcel Mauss*, trans. Felicity Baker (London: Routledge, 1987), p. 64.

94. Jacques Derrida, *Margins of Philosophy*, trans. Alan Bass (Chicago: University of Chicago Press, 1972), p. 65.

95. Foucault, *Archaeology of Knowledge*, p. 209.

CHAPTER THREE: PHILOSOPHICAL ARCHAEOLOGY

1. Immanuel Kant, *Theoretical Philosophy after 1781*, trans. Gary Hatfield (Cambridge, UK: Cambridge University Press, 2002), pp. 417 and 419.

2. *Ibid.*, p. 419.

3. *Ibid.*, p. 417.

4. *Ibid.*, p. 419.

5. Immanuel Kant, *Logic*, trans. Robert S. Hartman and Wolfgang Schwarz (New York: Dover, 1974), p. 29.

6. Immanuel Kant, *Philosophische Enzyklopädie*, in *Gesammelte Schriften, Akademie-Ausgabe* (Berlin: De Gruyter, 1973), vol. 29, p. 7.

7. *Ibid.*

8. Michel Foucault, "Nietzsche, Genealogy, History," in *Aesthetics, Method, and Epistemology*, trans. Robert Hurley (New York: New Press, 1998), p. 370.

9. *Ibid.*, pp. 373, 376.

10. *Ibid.*, p. 371.

11. *Ibid.*, pp. 372, 373.

12. Michel Foucault, *Dits et écrits*, ed. Daniel Defer and François Ewald (Paris: Gallimard, 1994), vol. 3, p. 147.

13. Franz Overbeck, *Kirchenlexicon Materialen: Christentum und Kultur*, ed. Barbara von Reibnitz, *Werke und Nachlass* (Stuttgart: Metzler, 1996), p. 53.

14. *Ibid.*, p. 57.

15. *Ibid.*, p. 53.

16. *Ibid.*, p. 55.

17. *Ibid.*, p. 53.

18. *Ibid.*, p. 54.

19. *Ibid.*, p. 52.

20. Martin Heidegger, *Being and Time*, trans. John Macquarrie and Edward Robinson (New York: Harper Perennial, 1962), p. 43.

21. Overbeck, *Kirchenlexicon*, p. 56.

22. Paolo Prodi, *Il sacramento del potere: Il giuramento politico nella storia costituzionale dell'Occidente* (Bologna: il Mulino, 1992), p. 24.

23. Georges Dumézil, *Mythe et épopée* (Paris: Gallimard, 1968), vol. 3, p. 14.

24. *Ibid.*

25. Antoine Meillet, *Linguistic historique et linguistic générale* (1921; Paris: Champion, 1975), p. 324.

26. *Ibid.*, vol. 1, p. 15.

27. Michel Foucault, *The Order of Things* (1994; New York: Vintage, 1970), p. xxii.

28. *Ibid.*, pp. xxi–xxii.

29. Michel Foucault, *The Archaeology of Knowledge*, trans. A. M. Sheridan Smith (New York: Pantheon Books, 1972), p. 191.

30. Marcel Mauss, *A General Theory of Magic*, trans. Robert Brain (London: Routledge and Kegan Paul, 1972), p. 118.

31. Henri Bergson, *Mind-Energy*, trans. H. Wilson Carr (New York: Palgrave Macmillan, 2007), p. 133.

32. Walter Benjamin, *The Arcades Project*, trans. Howard Eiland and Kevin McLaughlin (Cambridge, MA: Harvard University Press,1982), p. 459.

33. Enzo Melandri, "Michel Foucault: L'espistemologia delle scienze umane," *Lingua e stile* 2.1 (1967), p. 78.

34. *Ibid.*, p. 96.

35. Paul Ricoeur, *Freud and Philosophy: An Essay on Interpretation*, trans. Denis Savage (New Haven, CT: Yale University Press, 1970), p. 445.

36. *Ibid.*, p. 446.

37. Friedrich Nietzsche, *Untimely Meditations*, trans. R. J. Hollingdale (Cambridge, UK: Cambridge University Press, 1997), p. 67.

38. Enzo Melandri, *La linea e il circolo: Studio logico-filosofico sull'analogia* (Macerata: Quodlibet, 2004), pp. 65–66.

39. *Ibid.*, p. 67.

40. Sigmund Freud, *Moses and Monotheism*, trans. Katherine Jones (New York: Vintage Books, 1937), p. 162.

41. *Ibid.*, p. 163.

42. Cathy Caruth, *Unclaimed Experience: Trauma, Narrative, and History* (Baltimore: Johns Hopkins University Press, 1996), pp. 17–18.

43. Foucault, *Dits et écrits*, vol. 1, pp. 69–70 and 73.

44. *Ibid.*, p. 111.

45. *Ibid.*, p. 100.

46. *Ibid.*, p. 109.

47. *Ibid.*, p. 116.

48. *Ibid.*

49. *Ibid.*, pp. 118, 117.

50. Paolo Virno, "Un dedalo di parole: Per un'analisi linguistica della metropoli," in *La città senza luoghi*, ed. Massimo Ilardi (Genoa: Costa & Nolan, 1990), p. 74.

51. Benjamin, *The Arcades Project*, p. 471.

52. Foucault, *Dits et écrits*, vol. 1, p. 99.

53. Hermann Usener, *Götternamen: Versuch einer Lehre von der religiösen Begriffsbildung* (Frankfurt: Klostermann, 2000), p. 5.

54. Dumézil, *Mythe et épopée*, vol. 1, p. 9.

Index of Names

Zone Books series design by Bruce Mau

Typesetting by Meighan Gale